Boston Harbor, 1775

Boston Town, 1775

BROWN PAPER SCHOOL

USKids History: Book of the American Revolution

Howard Egger-Bovet *and* Marlene Smith-Baranzini, *writers*

Bill Sanchez, *illustrator*

James J. Rawls, *consulting editor*

Little, Brown and Company

Boston   New York   Toronto   London

A Yolla Bolly Press Book

USKids History: Book of the American Revolution was edited and prepared for publication at The Yolla Bolly Press, Covelo, California. The series is under the supervision of James Robertson and Carolyn Robertson. Production staff: Diana Fairbanks, Renée Menge, and Alexandra Chappell. Composition by Wilsted & Taylor, Oakland, California.

Acknowledgments

The authors wish to express their appreciation to James Rawls, professor of history at Diablo Valley College, California, for his assistance in the planning of this book, and for his review of the manuscript. Thanks also to the American Philosophical Society for permission to reprint the portrait of Benjamin Franklin on page 55.

FIRST EDITION

ISBN: 0-316-96922-2 (hc)
ISBN: 0-316-22204-6 (pb)
HC: 10 9 8 7 6 5 4 3 2 1
PB: 10 9 8 7 6 5 4 3 2 1

MV-NY

Published simultaneously in Canada by Little, Brown & Company (Canada) Limited

Printed in the United States of America

Library of Congress Cataloging-in-Publication Data

Egger-Bovet, Howard.
    Book of the American Revolution / written by Howard Egger-Bovet and Marlene Smith-Baranzini : illustrated by Bill Sanchez. — 1st ed.
        p.   cm. — (USKids history)
    Summary: Highlights the events leading up to the Revolutionary War, life in the colonies during wartime, and important figures of the time. Includes ideas for related activities.
    ISBN 0-316-96922-2
    1. United States—History—Revolution, 1775–1783—Juvenile literature.   [1. United States—History—Revolution, 1775–1783.]
I. Smith-Baranzini, Marlene.
II. Sanchez, Bill, ill.   III. Title.
IV. Series.
E208.E42   1994
973.7—dc20   93-21769

Contents

The Drummer Boy 7

Anger in Boston 9
Boston: An English Town
The Mystery of Yankee Doodle
What Is Red, Hot, and Itchy?
The Militia Helped the British Army
Why Red?
A Government to Please the King
The Hard Life of the British Soldier
Big Ideas at the Coffeehouse

I Have Rights 13
The Right Stuff

The Colonies, 1775 14

Revolutionary Body Parts: A Game 15

Casting Cannons in the Shadows 16
Growing Up at the Ironworks
How Ironworks Work
Make a Paper Quilt
The Pattern of Independence

The Moonlight Shepherd 19

The Story of John Robinson and the Polly 21
Two Kinds of Smugglers

Catch a Tea Smuggler 22
Mean Captain John Malcolm

Tax and Be Taxed: Two Games 24
A Strange Parade

The Sons of Liberty 26
Member Medals
The Man of the Revolution
The Stamp Act Congress
The Sons of Liberty Were Spreading

The Boston Massacre: A Play 28
A Bitter Brew
Tea Facts

Grandfather Peck's Tea Party 32
Did You Know?
An Englishman Praises the Tea Dumping
We Will Survive
The King Punishes Boston
The First Continental Congress
Adams's New Clothes
A Tireless Messenger for the Sons of Liberty
Telling It Like It Is

Spy Stories 36
Paul Revere's Thieves
Coffee, Tea, or Trouble?
Doctor Spy
Doctor Church's Code

British Spy: A Board Game 40

Secret Messages 42
One If By Land, Two If By Water

Boston, Lexington, and Concord, 1775 42

The First Battles 43

The War Begins 45

Joseph Palmer's Alarm 46
Committees of Correspondence
Colonial Newspapers

What Joseph Palmer Wrote 47
Colonial Newspapers
The News Arrives

The Battle of Breed's Hill 48
Front Row Seats
The Bigger Hill Gets the Credit

6

Daniel Boone Moves West   50
No Trespassing
Build a Fort

The Wilderness Road to Fort Boonesborough   53

Benjamin Franklin: Runaway Genius   54

The Inventor   55
The Leather Apron Club

Benjamin's Acrostic   56

The Story of Phillis Wheatley   57
Sir [George Washington]
A Hymn to the Evening, by Phillis Wheatley
Freedom, But Not for All

Tom Paine's Little Book   59
Thomas Paine

Brother Benjamin: A Game   60

Words to Change the World   61
Who Was This Man Jefferson?

The Colonies Vote for Freedom   63

The First Fourth of July   64

Old Glory Ice Cream   66
The Printer Was a Lady

Independence Day Noisemakers   67
Lost and Found: An Original Copy

The Beating of the Distant Drum   68
Sarah Spoke "Plain" English
What Did Sarah Wear?

Joseph Plumb Martin Goes to War   72
Joseph's Silver Dollar
An Army of Volunteers

New Shirts and Old Weapons
Please Pass the Flour

One Hard Winter   77
A Soldier's Iron Bondage
A Doctor's Diary

General in the Storm: A Game   80
The British March to New York
The Continental Army Attacks
The Soup That Won the War

America's First Flags   82
The Mystery of the First Flag
The British Plan for Victory
Design Your Flag

Pirates for Hire   84
Privateer Wages
Aboard a Privateer
A Just Prize
What Became of Israel Trask
Nothing But Pirates

The Amazing *Turtle*   88

Women in Battle   89

Victory at Yorktown   90
James Armistead Lafayette
The Youngest Major General

The World Turned Upside Down   92

If You Want to Know More   94

Index   96

Note: Activities and games are italicized.

The Drummer Boy

On the cover of this book is a picture of a drummer boy. He was about your age when he took part in one of the most important battles of the American Revolutionary War. We don't know his name. All we know is that he was there. We'll call him Oliver. Oliver was English. He probably came to America in about 1777, with his older brother who was a British soldier. They were sent by King George III to fight the rebellious colonists. They came on a sailing ship with several hundred other soldiers. The trip across the Atlantic Ocean was long—almost four weeks—and extremely uncomfortable. The quarters were cramped and the food was awful. Oliver was glad when the ship finally docked at New York.

It was not unusual for boys like Oliver to accompany a father or older brother to war. There were many jobs a boy could do for the army. Boys helped the cooks and took care of the animals. In battle, they carried water to thirsty soldiers, and they sometimes took them fresh gunpowder. Often the battlefields were so noisy and smoky that the officers in command could not tell what was happening at the far ends of their battle lines. Boys like Oliver were sometimes asked to run messages: orders to advance or to retreat, to begin or cease firing. Oliver was a fast runner, and he was brave. Though he took many chances, he was never wounded.

Each army had drummers and buglers and fife players. It was believed that the sound of stirring music gave the soldiers courage and lifted their spirits. Near the end of the war, the drummer for Oliver's regiment was wounded and could not march. Many soldiers were sick or had been killed. Reinforcements had not arrived. The English commander knew he must surrender. He asked Oliver to march with an officer through the battlefield to the American side. Oliver was to lead, drumming as he went, and the officer would march behind, carrying a white flag—the sign of surrender. Alone, the two of them would face the American artillery and riflemen. It was a dangerous task. There was always the chance the Americans might mistake their approach for a trick and fire on them.

You will read about Oliver's last battle in this book. You will also read about other children and men and women whose lives were changed by the war against England. It was the war that established the thirteen colonies as free and independent states. It made all the colonists free of the rule of a distant king. It was also the war that made *you* free, so you ought to know something about it. That is what history is all about. After all, you can't know where you are going if you don't know where you have been.

Oliver was a fast runner.

They stuck their heads out into the wet, salty Boston air.

Anger in Boston

He shouted at the British soldier who was approaching.

"Bloodyback! Lobsterback!"

"Yankee Doodle!"

Thomas dropped his wooden top. Harriet clutched her doll. They bounced off their beds and unlatched the window, sticking their heads out into wet, salty Boston air.

Below, in the rain, stood a man named John White. The raindrops found their way into the holes of his three-cornered hat and the rips of his tight-fitting brown jacket and breeches. He paid it no bother. He stood with his square-toed shoes firmly planted on the narrow cobblestone street and shouted at the British soldier who was approaching.

It was easy to spot a British soldier. His red woolen overcoat and tall, egg-shaped, bearskin hat could be seen from quite a distance.

The soldier was glad it was raining. The tight, white knee breeches he was wearing didn't cut off the circulation in his legs as much when they were wet. And they were wet. His entire uniform was soaked.

"Bloodyback!" shouted John White once more as he stood in the soldier's way.

A Crowd Gathers

Harriet and Thomas looked on as if they were watching a play from a balcony.

"Lobsterback!" shouted Thomas. Both children ducked down beneath the window.

"There's no need to hide," instructed John White, looking up. "He knows what he is."

"Get out of my way, Yankee Doodle," said the soldier, wiping the rain from his face. "I don't have time to harm you."

The growing commotion caused neighbors to leave their fireplaces to investigate the disturbance. Windows and doors opened. The audience grew.

Children ran out to tease the soldier. The children tugged at his overcoat and asked for money. The soldier did not glare at them. His stiff collar prevented him from looking down that far.

Boston: An English Town

By 1763 Boston had over forty-two streets with more than three thousand houses made of wood and brick. There were hundreds of shops, in which craftsmen made everything from chairs to anchors.

Along the cobblestone streets people entered English-like taverns and heard the sound of many languages being spoken. They sat in coffeehouses, reading books by English and French authors. Wealthy colonists followed English fashion. Men wore embroidered waistcoats and ruffled shirts. Women wore gowns and traveled in open horse-drawn carriages. One visitor to Boston claimed that it was "more like an English town than any in America."

The Mystery of Yankee Doodle

Yankee Doodle went to town
A-riding on a pony.
Stuck a feather in his hat
And called it macaroni.

Everyone is familiar with these words. They come from the song "Yankee Doodle," but what do the words mean? The word *yankee* came from the Scottish *yankie*, which meant a dishonest person. The word *doodle* was English slang for fool. Put the two words together and *yankee doodle* means a dishonest fool.

In the mid-1700s the English were in love with Italian food, especially macaroni. In 1775 Edward Bang added the famous line to the song, "stuck a feather in his hat and called it macaroni." Mr. Bang was teasing the British. He was saying they would do anything, no matter how silly, to make themselves look fashionable.

All he wanted was to get on his way.

"What's your hurry?" teased John White.

"You bloodybacks are so busy, protecting us. And when your duties are finished you take our jobs, when you're not stealing from us. Which are you up to today?"

You're a Yankee Doodle!

"Let me be. I have work at the docks."

"Work at the docks?" cried John White, taking off his hat and slapping it against his leg in disgust. "Do you hear that? You already have a job. The king pays you."

"Not enough," said a soldier.

"And what about me? I have a family. I don't have a job and you have two."

"Pity the poor redcoat," teased one of the men leaving his doorstep. "He has only one set of clothes. Poor man has to work in his uniform."

The men moved in. The soldier placed his hand on his bayonet. Thomas and Harriet's father, Benjamin Ward, had been watching from his door. He moved away from his wife and out into the rain to calm his neighbors.

"This talk will not make what is unfair fair," said Benjamin Ward, stepping in between the men and the soldier. "Your only accomplishment, I fear, will be a nasty cold. I say let him pass."

"You're right," replied John White, shaking his head. "Please pass with my blessing," he said, winking at his friends. The crowd stepped aside and let the soldier pass.

When he was four houses away, John White picked up loose pieces of cobblestone and threw them at the moving red target. The children followed suit. The soldier ignored the mistreatment. He had suffered worse punishment. He kept on walking. He needed the work more than he needed to fight.

"Someday," shouted John White, "it won't be stones we'll be hitting you with, but musket balls!"

"Let me be. I have work at the docks."

Why Red?

In battle, British soldiers marched in tightly packed ranks or lines. When a soldier was hit by a musket ball, his red overcoat made it difficult for others to know he was bleeding. This helped to stop those who were scared from running away.

It helped, but it didn't restrain everyone. Soldiers did desert their posts. Unfortunately for them, their red uniforms made it easy for an officer to spot them.

WHAT IS RED, HOT, AND ITCHY?

Wearing a British uniform was not pleasant. It was made of heavy wool, and it was hot in summer and itchy in winter.

The red overcoat fit tightly and was decorated like a birthday cake with piping, lace, and buttons of pewter or brass. An "X" was made across the soldier's chest by two belts. The belts held a bayonet and a cartridge box.

Under the overcoat was a vest of red or white. The white breeches were so tight they had to be put on wet. The boots were knee-length. The tall hat was heavy and had no brim to keep the sun out of the eyes.

The knapsack and other gear that each soldier carried weighed 125 pounds. The knapsack contained extra clothing, food, a blanket, and a tent. Other gear included a fourteen-pound musket, a bayonet, several pounds of musket balls, and a shovel. And to make sure the soldier stood straight, he had to wear a very stiff white collar.

THE MILITIA HELPED THE BRITISH ARMY

The British king allowed each colonial government to form a militia. The militia was a military organization made up of regiments, companies, and officers. Its duty was to assist the British army.

The colonial militia wasn't a professional army. The militiamen didn't have uniforms. Most men wore a three-cornered hat, a home-made hunting shirt, and gray or brown trousers called "breeches." They also had to provide their own muskets and knives, make their own musket balls, and bring whatever else they needed from home.

Militiamen were given little training. Occasionally regiments would meet at the town green, where an officer would try to teach his men British battle formations. Training wasn't taken very seriously. Officers didn't demand discipline from their men because they were all friends.

A Government to Please the King

The colonies had three kinds of government: royal, corporate, and proprietary. Most of the colonies, including South Carolina, were royal governments. They were ruled by the king. Corporate colonies were governed by English businessmen under a grant from the king. Proprietary colonies were governed by an individual under a grant from the king. Massachusetts colony was both a corporate and a royal government! No wonder colonists were puzzled by each other's governments.

How a Royal Government Worked

Royal colonies were governed by a legislature that worked like the British Parliament. The Parliament was made up of two groups and the king. The colonial legislature had an assembly, a council, and a governor.

Men were elected to the colonial assembly. The assembly's job was to create and agree on bills, or proposals, that should become law. A bill, for example, could call for a new road to be built.

When the assembly agreed on a bill, it was sent to the council, whose members were appointed by the king. If they agreed to the bill, it was sent to the governor. If the governor approved the bill, he signed it. The bill became law and was sent to the king for final approval.

Since the governor was appointed by the king, he approved only those bills that pleased the king. This rarely pleased the legislature.

THE HARD LIFE OF THE BRITISH SOLDIER

In the 1700s, Britain's cities were swamped with poor people living in crowded slums. Riots occurred regularly. Stealing was commonplace.

The British soldier in the story "Anger in Boston" had wanted to be a farmer, but the landowners refused to rent him a plot of land. They could make more money using the land to raise sheep.

The soldier went to London, but he couldn't find work. He started stealing from shops. One day he was caught.

He was taken before a judge and given two choices: hang or join the British army. The choice was easy, but it wasn't an enjoyable decision.

The British soldier was expected to look like a picture. He spent three hours dressing. The clothing was uncomfortable. Inspections were frequent. If a soldier broke a rule, he was whipped. A man could be given up to a thousand lashings at a time.

Many British soldiers served in the colonies—but life wasn't any better there. Soldiers made two cents a day. From this tiny wage were subtracted charges for anything from musket repair to medicine.

There was no way a soldier could support his family without taking a second job, or stealing. Many colonial employers were eager to hire British soldiers. It made them feel safe knowing a soldier was working for them.

Unfortunately, the more jobs British soldiers took, the fewer jobs were available for colonists like John White.

BIG IDEAS AT THE COFFEEHOUSE

To the coffeehouse! That's where merchants and carpenters, bankers and glass blowers gathered to sit around tables, sip coffee, and argue.

In Europe, people went to coffeehouses to talk about the latest novel, such as *Robinson Crusoe*. They argued about the rights of people and whether a king was necessary. You name the topic, the coffeehouses were serving it up.

In the colonies, coffeehouses were just as popular. The thoughts consuming Europeans also consumed the colonists. The Europeans' bold discussion of rights gave colonists the courage to talk of independence. Their words and thoughts fed the imagination of colonists who went to bed and dreamed of freedom.

They argued about the rights of people.

I Have Rights

It is recess at school. John pushes Billy. Billy pushes John. The teacher on duty walks over to find out what the problem is. When the teacher asks Billy for an explanation he says, "John pushed me. So I had the right to push him back, and I did."

What does Billy mean by "I had the right"? What is a right, anyway? The word *right* has many definitions. Right can mean correct, as in the right answer. But in this case right has a different meaning. Right means a claim, something a person deserves to be able to do. Billy feels he deserves to be able to push John, since John pushed him. The teacher doesn't agree that pushing back is a right. She recommends other solutions. Do you think pushing back is a right?

In the 1700s people were concerned with rights. This time in history has been named the Age of Enlightenment. It could have been called the Age of Questions. People were no longer satisfied with just working and sleeping. They wanted to know about the world they lived in. Give me a question, a puzzling, head-scratching question!

Why does a ripe apple fall from a tree instead of float toward the clouds? What is air made of? People asked themselves what they wanted from their lives, what they deserved in life. From these kinds of questions came the belief that every person, whether he had money or not, had rights no one could take away.

Kids' Rights

Do kids have rights that no one can take away? For example:

Do kids have the right to be loved?

Do kids have the right to be safe from abuse by an adult?

Do kids have the right to be taught subjects only kids are interested in?

Do kids have the right to keep secrets from their parents?

Do kids have the right to live in a safe environment?

Do kids have the right to eat as much food as they want?

Get together with friends and come up with a list of "kids' rights." Take these rights and turn them into short statements, or slogans, that communicate those "kids' rights" you believe in. For instance: Do kids have the right to eat as much food as they want? If you think that this is a "right," then come up with a short phrase that tells people what you think. How about: *It's my right to have a huge appetite.*

As a kid, no one understands your concerns better than you. It is up to you to stand up for your rights. Colonists also realized that they had to stand up for their rights, whether the king liked it or not!

THE RIGHT STUFF

Once you have your slogan based on "kids' rights," you can present it separately on a T-shirt, a flag, or a poster.

What You Need:

T-shirt: fabric paints, a white cotton T-shirt, and several brushes.

Flag: a dowel or stick, a white sheet or construction paper, and paints. The sheet or paper can be nailed or stapled to the dowel.

Poster: posterboard, crayons or marking pens, glitter, and decorative stickers. Display them proudly. It's your right.

Before painting on a T-shirt, you should put a piece of cardboard between the front and the back, to prevent paint from going through and to make a smooth surface to paint on. You may also use clothespins to pin back the sleeves, so they don't get accidentally painted.

14

The Colonies, 1775

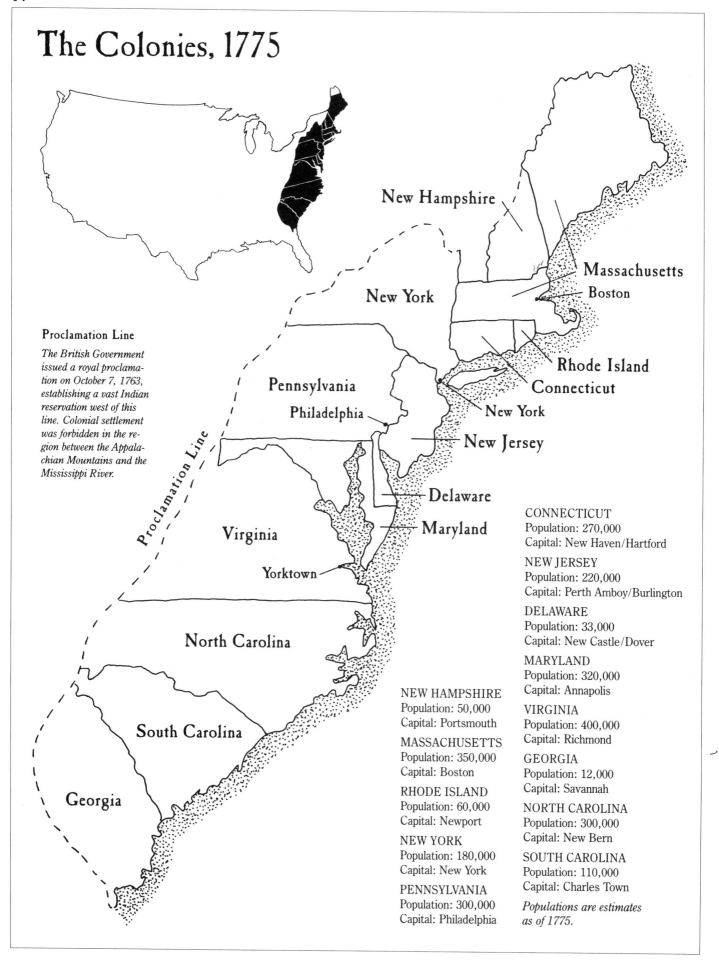

New Hampshire

Massachusetts
Boston

New York

Rhode Island
Connecticut

New York

New Jersey

Proclamation Line

The British Government issued a royal proclamation on October 7, 1763, establishing a vast Indian reservation west of this line. Colonial settlement was forbidden in the region between the Appalachian Mountains and the Mississippi River.

Pennsylvania

Philadelphia

Delaware

Maryland

Virginia

Yorktown

North Carolina

South Carolina

Georgia

CONNECTICUT
Population: 270,000
Capital: New Haven/Hartford

NEW JERSEY
Population: 220,000
Capital: Perth Amboy/Burlington

DELAWARE
Population: 33,000
Capital: New Castle/Dover

MARYLAND
Population: 320,000
Capital: Annapolis

VIRGINIA
Population: 400,000
Capital: Richmond

GEORGIA
Population: 12,000
Capital: Savannah

NORTH CAROLINA
Population: 300,000
Capital: New Bern

SOUTH CAROLINA
Population: 110,000
Capital: Charles Town

NEW HAMPSHIRE
Population: 50,000
Capital: Portsmouth

MASSACHUSETTS
Population: 350,000
Capital: Boston

RHODE ISLAND
Population: 60,000
Capital: Newport

NEW YORK
Population: 180,000
Capital: New York

PENNSYLVANIA
Population: 300,000
Capital: Philadelphia

Populations are estimates as of 1775.

Revolutionary Body Parts: A Game

Do you know the location of the thirteen colonies? Here's a game that will stretch your body and your knowledge.

What You Need:

Two to four players; a flat, outside surface; chalk, a pen or pencil; scissors; cardboard.

1. Make playing cards by cutting the cardboard into thirteen 3-inch squares.

2. Write one direction listed below on each card:

Place your right hand on New Hampshire.
Place your left foot on Massachusetts.
Place your right hand on Rhode Island.
Place your left hand on Connecticut.
Place your left foot on New York.
Place your right hand on Pennsylvania.
Place your right foot on New Jersey.
Place your left hand on Delaware.
Place your left foot on Maryland.
Place your right hand on Virginia.
Place your right foot on North Carolina.
Place your left hand on South Carolina.
Place your left foot on Georgia.

3. Draw the thirteen colonies on an outside surface using a piece of chalk, and a map of the colonies as a guide. Practice drawing the colonies using paper and pencil first. When you're ready, draw a 5-foot square on a surface outside. Draw the colonies within this space.

Your drawing doesn't have to be perfect, but it is important to make sure the small colonies, like Rhode Island, are drawn smaller than the large colonies, like Pennsylvania.

How to Play:

Choose one person to shuffle and select the cards. The other player stands outside the colonies and waits to hear the instructions.

As each card is read the player attempts to touch the colony with a body part. Players can touch a colony only with their hands or feet, as instructed on the cards.

If Two People Are Playing:

When the first player falls over, the number of colonies touched by the player is added up. The players switch roles. The game continues until that person falls. The number of colonies touched are added up. The player who has touched the most colonies wins.

If Four People Are Playing:

One person reads the cards. Three people play. The first person to fall switches places with the person reading the cards. When the next person falls, it is his or her turn to read the cards. Only two players remain. The game continues until one player is left standing. That player is the winner.

Note: If a card's instruction is "Place your right hand on Virginia," and a player already has his or her right hand on Virginia, another card is selected. Also, when all the cards have been read once, reshuffle the deck and start again.

ADAM—
PLACE YOUR
RIGHT HAND
ON PENNSYL-
VANIA!

Casting Cannons in the Shadows

Men came running from the nearby village.

The bell rang. Men came running from the nearby village. It was time. The molten iron was about to be tapped from the furnace.

Inside the ironworks, Jonathan, a nine-year-old apprentice, stood hypnotized by the red glow from the hot blast furnace. Beads of sweat rolled down his face as a sample of molten iron rolled out of the furnace and into one of the bar-shaped molds, or patterns, in the sand.

"Jonathan," shouted his father, "don't look at the river of iron. Look at what I'm doing with it, if you want to be a fine molder. You must guide the liquid iron, but you must be careful not to let any sand get into the mold."

Jonathan's entire family worked for the ironworks. His mother worked as a cook for the owner. His sister, who was eight years old, worked as a maid.

It was a good life, but it was also a life of crime. According to British law, anyone who worked in an ironworks in the colonies was a criminal.

British law forbade colonists from setting up ironworks. Colonists could only dig the iron ore and ship it to Great Britain. There it would be smelted and formed into tools, and then shipped back for colonists to purchase.

The colonists scorned this law and any talk of trying to close down the colonial ironworks. It was not reasonable to wait for British ships to bring finished ironware to the colonies when they could make it faster and cheaper in North America.

Jonathan turned away from his father and stared at the furnace. When he looked back his father was gone. He spotted a single stream of molten iron flowing away from the other molds. The liquid iron traveled into the shadows. It was there that Jonathan found his father.

The molten iron had collected in a crucible, or large kettle. His father dipped a long-handled ladle into the pool of liquid metal. He carefully poured it into one of two molds. Jonathan had never seen these molds before. They were shaped somewhat like two halves of a pear.

"What are you making?" asked Jonathan.

"I'm making a cannon," replied his father softly. "If you watch nothing else I do, watch me now. We may be making more cannons than stoves someday soon."

GROWING UP AT THE IRONWORKS

The ironworks wasn't just a place where iron and iron products were manufactured. It was a village. There were houses for the workers. There was a store where people bought goods, and a farm that produced food and raised animals.

Jonathan and his sister were born in the village. They played with other children. But when the village children reached the age of eight, they began apprenticeships in which they learned how to do jobs.

Like other boys, Jonathan was taught how to do his father's job. Girls assisted their mothers at home. Some mothers were employed by the owner of the ironworks. They cooked for the owner's family and cleaned their large home.

Jonathan's mother was a cook. She brought Jonathan's sister along and taught her how to be a housecleaner. The work day was long. Jonathan and his sister sometimes labored twelve hours a day.

It is not certain whether girl apprentices were paid, but boys were usually paid for any iron product they made. The parents controlled any wages boys made.

There wasn't a school in the village. Some parents joined together, if they had the money, and hired a tutor to come and teach their children to read and write—when they weren't working.

When Jonathan and his sister became adults they could leave the ironworks. But there was little reason to leave. The ironworks offered work, a place to live, family, and friends.

How Ironworks Work

Many workers were needed to run an ironworks. Miners dug up the iron ore, which they washed in nearby streams. Charcoal, to heat the furnace, did not come in a bag. It had to be made.

Men chopped and stacked wood in a conelike shape, then covered it with sticks and layers of leaves. A chimney was made in the cone and a fire was started and kept smoldering for two weeks. This low heat burned the wood slowly and removed the water. After two weeks the wood became charcoal.

Fillers then loaded the ironworks' furnace with charcoal, limestone, and iron ore, and ignited it. Every half-hour the furnace was refilled with charcoal, until it was hot enough to melt the iron ore.

The molten metal sank to the bottom of the furnace, where a worker either guided the liquid metal into a crucible, or into bar-shaped molds near the furnace. From the crucible, workers used long-handled ladles to scoop out the liquid and pour it into molds.

When the hot metal cooled, the molded metal was removed, and items such as handles could be added. The metal that was shaped into bars was transported to a foundry. The bars were heated and hammered to get rid of the metal's flaws. This made them strong enough to be made into tools.

"I'm making a cannon," his father replied softly.

THE PATTERN OF INDEPENDENCE

No colonial home was without quilts, because no home was without drafts. Mary's house was filled with quilts. There were quilts hanging over chairs. There was a quilt on every bed. The cedar chest was filled with seven quilts, or was it eight? Quilts kept people warm throughout the bitter winter nights and provided entertainment as women sat making new ones all year round.

During the evening, when it was cold, Mary sat by her mother and watched her make a quilt by the light of the fire. Mary was amazed at how small her mother made her stitches as she created a quilt pattern over the fine English fabric. Mary loved to touch the material. It felt so smooth in her hands. She adored staring at the printed picture in the quilt's center and dreaming.

But when Mary's mother ran out of material this time, she didn't ask Mary to go to the store to purchase more English fabric. Instead, Mary and her mother searched the house for worn-out clothes, tablecloths, any piece of cloth, and collected them in a sack. It was more fun than going to the store. Mary felt as if she and her mother were hunting, just like her father and brother did.

At night Mary and her mother emptied the sack on the floor. Out poured their catch of cloth, shirts, sheets, and pants. They examined each item, cutting out any pieces of usable material.

Mary watched as her mother cut these pieces into triangles, squares, and circles. She sewed the shapes together in a pattern, creating a cover for a new quilt. It wasn't like any quilt her mother had made before.

One afternoon, women arrived and gathered on the porch to work on her mother's new quilt. Mary carefully listened to the women talk. They weren't buying English fabric either. One woman stated she'd never need English fabric again. She had plenty of scraps to make her quilts.

Another woman spoke of not buying any British goods. She said it was the only way to make the king listen to the colonists. Mary said nothing. She didn't understand much of what the women were saying.

Her mother told the other women that she called her quilt pattern the "pattern of independence." They nodded in approval. Mary hugged her mom gently. She adored her mother's new quilt.

Make a Paper Quilt

Got some free wall space and some time? Why not make a colonial paper quilt?

What You Need:

A piece of white paper 12 inches by 12 inches square, some smaller pieces of paper to work out your ideas, a ruler and pencil, scissors, crayons, markers, or colored pencils, and tape.

1. Using a ruler and pencil, work out a geometric quilt pattern (see illustrations for ideas) on your small paper. Imagine how many different patterns are possible!

2. Duplicate the pattern you like on your 12-inch-square paper. Color in the different areas to look like fabric. Some shapes are solid colors, some can have patterns, stripes, or dots. You could even use wrapping paper or colored paper to decorate your quilt design.

If you liked making this, you and some friends could make sixteen blocks and tape them together to make a 4-foot-square quilt!

The Moonlight Shepherd

"Wake up, William. You've got to move the sheep down the road."

"Wake up, William," his mother said, leaning over his bed.

"What . . . ," shouted William.

"Shhhh," his mother said, "you'll wake your little sister. I don't want her to know you've been out of bed, just in case someone asks tomorrow."

"About what? What are you talking about?" insisted William.

"I can't tell you anything. It's for your own safety," said his mother. "Get dressed. You've got to move the sheep down to the road."

"And what do I do with them when I reach the road?" William asked.

"Take them down to the bend in the road. Then walk them back and do it one more time, just to be sure."

"That's several miles at least," William moaned.

"Yes, I know. Stop wasting time and get going, William, please."

"Why not get John to do it?" William asked.

"Your brother is already doing it. He's moving sheep up the road," responded his mother.

The moonlight shining through the window revealed the serious look on his mother's face. William said nothing more. He got dressed and gathered the sheep. His mother had told him not to carry a lantern, as he might be seen. The moon's light would have to do.

When he reached the road, he did as his mother instructed him. Suddenly he heard a noise. Ahead he saw the silhouette of sheep coming toward him.

He halted his sheep and slowly walked on. The other shepherd came toward William.

"It's you, Samuel," said William, breathing a sigh of relief.

"Gave you a scare?" Samuel chuckled.

"I suppose," William admitted. "What are you doing out here this time of night?"

"I could ask you the same question."

"I cannot say," William stated.

"Me neither," said Samuel.

"What do you think this is all about?" William asked.

"I think I know," Samuel said, lowering his voice. "I've noticed wagon wheel tracks on the road. And earlier, I saw the lights of a ship."

"What do you think was on the wagons?" William asked.

"I bet barrels of molasses, judging from the barrels I saw in our cellar."

"It must be smuggled molasses," William added.

"We'd better get back to work," advised Samuel.

William started back to his flock.

"William," whispered Samuel, "make sure you cover up the wagon tracks."

"I will," promised William.

"What do you think was on those wagons?"

The Story of John Robinson and the "Polly"

Captain Ayers was a smuggler. His ship was anchored in Newport Harbor. He stepped onto the dock and walked toward the customs agent, reaching for some gold coins in his pockets. Ayers had never seen this agent before.

"Hello, Sir. Captain Ayers at your service. My ship, the *Polly*, is at anchor in the harbor."

"Good evening to you, Sir," said customs agent John Robinson.

"I've not seen you before," stated the captain.

"Excuse my rudeness. I have just started my duties here in Newport. My name is John Robinson."

John Robinson was an unusual kind of customs agent. He was honest. He would not accept bribe money from smugglers.

"I am here to enforce the king's new law, the Sugar Act," stated Robinson. "The law says to collect all the duty on any molasses, sugar, or rum you have on board. And so I will. Tell me what you are carrying and the exact amount of your cargo."

"I'd be glad to," replied the captain, letting the coins in his hand fall back into his pocket. "I'm carrying sixty-three barrels of molasses."

(In truth there was triple that number on his ship.)

"That is the total, Sir?" asked John Robinson.

"To the last barrel," answered Captain Ayers.

"All right then, follow me to the duty house. You will pay duty on sixty-three barrels of molasses. Are you planning to unload the *Polly* here?"

"No, Sir, I'm heading up the coast to Dighton," responded the captain.

A short time later, the captain set sail for Dighton. He was pleased. The new agent may have asked too many questions, but he didn't ask for money. So much the better.

After the *Polly* departed, John Robinson decided something was wrong. Sixty-three barrels was too small a cargo for such a large ship. He cursed himself for not having searched the ship, but it was still not too late. He decided to enlist the British warship *Maidstone* to take him north after the *Polly*.

The *Maidstone* overtook the *Polly* at sea.

"Prepare to be boarded!" shouted John Robinson.

John Robinson boarded the *Polly* with a guard of armed soldiers. The *Polly's* crew could do nothing but watch.

Robinson discovered the captain had lied to him. The agent seized the ship. He left two people to guard the *Polly* and returned to Rhode Island to find a crew to bring the *Polly* back. But the two guards grew thirsty and went ashore.

As evening approached, the *Polly's* crew returned, boarded the vessel, and removed everything from the ship, even the sails!

When John Robinson returned, he found the *Polly* beached and badly damaged. A sheriff arrested Robinson for allowing the ship to be abused. Later, from jail, he wrote to a friend in Newport asking for help, adding, "I continue ready to suffer happy in the comfort that I am doing my duty."

Help finally came and John Robinson was released. The battered *Polly* was seized as the king's property and towed back to Newport. But the property was worthless. After all Robinson's effort, the smugglers had gotten away with their smuggled molasses.

Two Kinds of Smugglers

Barrels of molasses were brought to the colonies by ships. Before the molasses was unloaded, the owner had to pay a duty, or fee, on every barrel. It was the law. This rule made Great Britain richer.

To enforce this law, the king appointed customs agents to collect duty from ships' captains. Some captains dodged paying duty. Such men were called smugglers.

They smuggled their cargo into the colonies in two ways. Some captains anchored their ships up the coast, away from the harbor and the customs agent. There they sold the illegal cargo to the colonists—at a profit. The colonists carted it away on wagons and hid the cargo in cellars.

Other smugglers docked their ships in the harbor and met with the customs agent. The smugglers knew the customs agent was paid only a small wage.

The smugglers gave the agent money. In return the agent collected none, or only a small portion, of the duty. Since all the duty the agent collected went to the king, many agents were happy to increase their small salary by taking bribes.

Catch a Tea Smuggler

Colonists despised paying a tax on tea. Was there a way around the tax? Yes. People smuggled the tea into the country to avoid the customs agents and the tax they charged.

Customs agents searched for smuggled goods. They looked in ships and houses. They also looked the other way, if a smuggler gave them a tempting enough bribe.

You can be that tea smuggler or customs agent, if you're up to a risky game of hide-and-seek.

What You Need:

Two or more players, cardboard, a pair of scissors, a pencil, and bribes.

1. Draw three letters in block form: "T," "E," and "A." The letters should be 3 inches high by 3 inches wide.

2. Cut the letters out.

How to Play:

Object of the game: The first agent that finds all three letters in ten minutes wins.

To begin, decide who will be the smuggler and who will be the customs agent. If more than two are playing, work in two teams. The smuggler must hide the letters in the house before the customs agent is allowed in. The three letters should be hidden separately and in no more than one room.

A bribe can be offered to the customs agent before or during the search. Before a bribe is offered, the smuggler must decide what he or she is willing to offer. This bribe must be written down. The customs agent must decide what kind of bribe is acceptable.

If a bribe is offered at the start of the search, and the agent accepts the bribe, the players switch roles. If the bribe is unacceptable to the customs agent, then all players must agree on one that is acceptable. If not, the search will continue.

If no bribe is offered, the agent searches the room for *ten minutes*. If the letters are not found, the players switch roles. However, if the letter "T" is found, the agent is given *ten extra minutes* to find the letters, after the first ten minutes have expired.

During the search, the smuggler has the right to distract the customs agent. Examples: He or she can give false information or tell jokes or turn on music.

The players continue to switch roles until someone finds all three letters.

Note: The smuggler can give a bribe only *one* time during the entire game. If the customs agent finds the letters, then the smuggler must pay double whatever the bribe was.

Possible bribes: candy bars, comic books, doing a person's chores on Saturday. If the customs agent finds the letters, but no bribe was ever offered, then the agent receives the bribe written down by the smuggler.

MAY 29, 1765: Patrick Henry Condemns British for Stamp Act. Virginia colonist Patrick Henry claimed British are levying illegal taxes in colonies. Colonists loyal to the king accused Henry of treason. Many colonists stopped buying British paper goods, now more costly because of the stamp tax.

MEAN CAPTAIN JOHN MALCOLM

Captain John Malcolm was a customs agent who collected his duties with a sword and a fist, never with courtesy. He was the kind of customs agent rebellious colonists loved to hate.

One winter day, in Boston, Captain Malcolm was cursing and waving his cane at a young boy. A man named George Hewes came by and asked Malcolm if he was going to hit the boy. Captain Malcolm argued with Mr. Hewes, then struck him in the head with his cane.

Later that evening, a crowd of angry colonists gathered around Malcolm's house. They raised a ladder up to his window. They broke the window and dragged Malcolm out to the street and into a cart.

He was stripped to his britches, driven through town in the cold night air, and then brought before a barrel of boiling tar. While sev-eral men held Captain Malcolm, someone dipped a mop into the hot, black tar and then swabbed it over his body.

Malcolm screamed as the hot tar burned his skin. Beside the cart, women split open pillows. The men in the cart raised the pillows above the captain's head and shook them. Feathers rained down upon him and stuck to his tarred skin.

Captain Malcolm's public torture was not over. Looking more like a chicken than a man, he was threatened with hanging if he did not give up his customs job. He refused, until some-one threatened to cut off his ears. After four hours of torture, he was brought home and rolled out of the cart, half-dead.

Captain John Malcolm recovered from his at-tack. He was fortunate. Many who were tarred and feathered went insane.

A mob forces John Malcolm into a cart. They will parade him around town before covering him with tar and feathers.

Tax and Be Taxed: Two Games

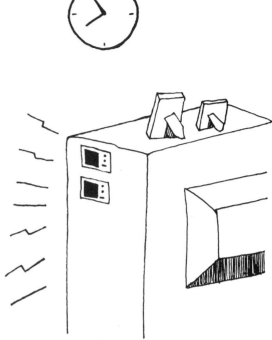

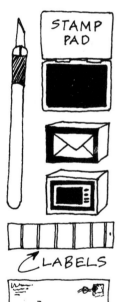

First, draw your designs onto art gum erasers. Next, with the help of an adult, cut the designs out, using the X-Acto knife. Press each design into a stamp pad, then onto peel-off labels. You can use these labels to tax and be taxed!

When the Stamp Act was passed by Parliament, it forced colonists to pay more for any printed matter. Stamps were placed on everything from newspapers to wills. This meant a tax was added to the price of the paper product. The tax increased British profits. It also increased the colonists' anger.

Now you have a chance to force a stamp tax on someone else, as well as to have a stamp tax forced upon you. Are you ready to tax and be taxed?

What You Need:

An adult, two art gum erasers, an ink pad, an X-Acto knife, and peel-off labels.

1. Design two stamps. The first is for the tax on watching television. Some possible designs are: an eye, a TV, a dime.

2. Carve your design into an eraser using an X-Acto knife. *Before* starting, tell an adult you are going to be using this knife. Remember, what you carve away will not show up when you ink the eraser and print your design. What you leave will show up.

Next, make a stamp for taxing the mail. Some possible designs are: a dime, a square with an "M" in the center, the outline of an envelope.

3. Test your stamps. Press the carved side of each eraser down on the ink pad, lift it up, and then press it down on a peel-off label.

4. Print your two stamps onto the peel-off labels. Ten or twenty of each should be enough.

A Tax on TV

In this game, you will be taxed one stamp (ten cents) for every hour of TV you watch. You pay the adult and that person puts the stamp on the side of the TV so you can keep track. At the end of each hour, the TV must be turned off unless you buy another stamp. No cheating. And you must buy stamps one at a time. Play this game for one week. During that time, the adult has the privilege of *raising the tax* once. If the tax goes to twenty cents, it takes *two* stamps to buy an hour's worth of TV.

A Tax on the Mail

Now it's your turn to get even. To play this game, you must collect and deliver the household mail. (Get the adult to agree to leave it in the box until you get home.) You may put one stamp on three pieces of mail (not all of it) so choose carefully. Don't deliver until the tax has been paid. If the tax is refused, that piece of mail doesn't get delivered. Play the game for one week. During that time, you may, if you choose, raise the tax to twenty cents (two stamps).

JULY 1765: Angry Colonists Organize Against High Taxes. In Boston, Philadelphia, and other towns, new radical groups called the "Sons of Liberty" and "Liberty Boys" vowed to fight recent taxes passed by Parliament.

A STRANGE PARADE

Down King Street the parade came, men holding sticks and women holding babies, waving their arms in anger, shouting, "Down with the doctor! A curse on the Stamp Act!"

The parade stopped before a gallows. Three life-size dolls were hoisted up and hung from the gallows. Fifteen feet above the platform the dolls slowly swayed.

"Who will come up and give these dolls a name?" challenged a man standing on the platform.

"I will," shouted a man pushing his way through the crowd.

The volunteer was handed a piece of paper and a quill pen. He dipped the pen into an inkwell and wrote on a scrap of paper, "THE STAMP MAN." He stuck the note on the doll's chest using a pin. In the doll's right hand he stuck a piece of paper that said, "THE STAMP ACT."

Another person from the crowd stepped onto the platform and attached a note to the second doll's chest which read, "WICKED, VILLAINOUS DOCTOR." On the third doll the final volunteer attached two notes. One note stated, "THAT FAWNING, FLATTERING, SCHEMING, SCOUNDREL MARTIN HOWARD." It was, as with the other two dolls, attached to this doll's chest. The second note was attached to the right arm with the message, "CURSED AMBITION AND YOUR CURSED CLAN HAS RUINED ME."

The writing was finished. The crowd broke into song, "All internal taxes let us nobly spurn. These effigies [images] first, the stamp papers burn."

Then the crowd set the gallows on fire. The flames quickly caught the images of Dr. Moffatt, Mr. Howard, and the stamp man. Soon nothing was left but ashes.

It was not over. As the sun was setting, the crowd went to Mr. Howard's home and destroyed it. They also sawed down trees and stuffed them into two cannons used during ceremonial parades. When there was nothing left to demolish, they went to Dr. Moffatt's house and did the same thing. The stamp officer, fearing for his home and his life, resigned from his job the next day.

This was how the Stamp Act was greeted when it became law on March 22, 1765. Colonists were enraged by the stamp tax. They believed only the colonies had the right to tax goods they made. The Stamp Act trespassed on the colonists' liberty.

Soon support in England for the Stamp Act began to fade. British merchants were losing money because colonial merchants refused to do business with them till the Stamp Act was repealed or canceled.

Colonists hated the Stamp Act. Their version of the stamp represented a curse upon the colonies.

The crowd set the gallows on fire.

The Sons of Liberty

"They take our money and our liberty."

Member Medals

All members of the Sons of Liberty wore a medal around their neck. On one side of the medal was the figure of a strong arm grasping a pole topped with a cap of liberty and surrounded by the words *Sons of Liberty*. On the other side was a representation of a Liberty Tree, an appointed tree under which rebellious colonists gathered to protest.

"What's the password?" asked John Taylor, standing behind the front door of his house.

"For the good of the colonies," said the man who was waiting to be let in.

The door opened and the man entered.

"Everybody is upstairs in the attic," said Taylor.

"All right," said Samuel Adams as the newcomer entered. "It's time to plan. New members of the tax board have arrived. We know why they are here, to take our money and liberty in the form of taxes. I say let's give them a Sons-of-Liberty welcome. On March 18 I want images made of these collectors. Take them to the Liberty Tree, hang them. Then burn them. Then pay a visit to their houses, just to scare them."

The Sons of Liberty carried out Adams's instructions. They awaited new orders. They did not have to wait long.

The *Liberty* had arrived in Boston Harbor. The *Liberty's* captain had lied about the amount of cargo on board ship. The less cargo the captain said he had, the less tax he'd have to pay.

Adams wanted the Sons of Liberty to unload the *Liberty's* cargo to show that the captain had been lying—and there was nothing any official could do about it.

British officials *did* do something about it. They had a British warship seize the *Liberty*.

The Sons of Liberty retaliated by dragging a customs agent's ship ashore and burning it. Adams quickly wrote a letter to the *Gazette* stating that the *Liberty* had been seized, "under a pretense of the law, at an unseasonable time, with the aid of a military power."

Adams did not mention that the ship's captain had lied. He painted a picture that showed the British had assaulted an innocent colonist.

No one could run a riot better than Samuel Adams.

THE MAN OF THE REVOLUTION

When Samuel Adams created the secret club called the Sons of Liberty, he was certain of one point. If his club started enough riots, Parliament wouldn't be able to ignore the colonists' anger over unfair laws.

It became a battle of wills between the Sons of Liberty and Parliament. Parliament kept passing unjust laws, and the Sons of Liberty met each law with riots.

This was getting nowhere. Samuel Adams knew what had to happen next. He was convinced the only way to stop Parliament's mistreatment of the colonies was to seek independence. The only way to gain independence was to fight for it. Later, Thomas Jefferson, the man who wrote the Declaration of Independence for the colonies, said Adams was "truly the Man of the Revolution."

This English political cartoon shows America in flames. The fire is being fed by members of Parliament, who continued to pass unfair laws. Some members of Parliament were sympathetic to the colonies and are shown trying to put the fire out.

THE STAMP ACT CONGRESS

The Stamp Act accomplished what nothing had before: It brought the colonies together. Before the Stamp Act, when an unfair law was passed, each colony wrote separate letters to Parliament expressing its opinion.

James Otis, of the Massachusetts legislature, offered another choice. He wanted the thirteen colonies to gather in New York and write one letter of protest instead of thirteen. He sent an invitation to each colonial assembly to send representatives to a Stamp Act Congress. A congress was more than just another meeting. It represented a pledge that the people were committed to working together to speak as one group, not as individuals.

James Otis's invitation made many men in the thirteen colonial assemblies uneasy. Until now, all orders passed by an assembly had to have the approval of the governor, who was loyal to the

king. To send men to this congress, where orders might be passed without the governor's approval, was against British law. Breaking British law was cause for being arrested.

The governors of Virginia, Maryland, North Carolina, and Georgia were very upset by Otis's suggestion; they kicked out all the men in their assemblies so they couldn't attend the Stamp Act Congress.

MARCH 5, 1770: Five Colonists Die in Riot. Armed British soldiers in Boston fired on a crowd of citizens tonight, killing five unarmed men. Huge crowds gathered in streets to taunt and tease soldiers when an unidentified British officer ordered the shooting. One officer and six soldiers were arrested and charged with five murders. Patriot Samuel Adams called killings a "massacre."

The Sons of Liberty Were Spreading

When the Stamp Act became law, mobs took to the streets in Boston. In Parliament, Colonel Isaac Barre, a friend of the colonists, called these mobs the "Sons of Liberty."

This title became the name of an organization dedicated to spreading rebellion throughout the colonies. Samuel Adams directed the founding chapter of the Sons of Liberty in Boston. Soon, there were chapters in New York Town [now New York City], New York; Philadelphia, Pennsylvania; New Haven and Hartford, Connecticut; and Providence, Rhode Island.

Throughout the colonies church bells rang out in protest. Crowds gathered under specific trees appointed "Liberty Trees." The crowds sang the latest protest songs and held rallies to encourage people not to buy British goods. Images of anyone in favor of the Stamp Act were burned. The most daring colonists dragged stamp officers, whose job it was to sell the stamps, out of their homes to be tortured and to watch their homes be destroyed.

The Boston Massacre: A Play

Note: The following play is based on a real event that happened in Boston, Massachusetts, on March 5, 1770.

Paul Revere's poster of the Boston Massacre, which showed the captain ordering his men to fire on a docile crowd, was a potent piece of colonial propaganda.

CAST OF CHARACTERS

Narrator
Sentry: a British soldier
Cloaked man: a member of the Sons of Liberty
Samuel Grey: a ropemaker
Soldier #1: a British soldier
John Grey: owner of ropeworks
A boy: son of a rebellious colonist
British officer

Captain Preston: officer in charge of British troops
Crispus Attucks: a runaway slave
Benjamin Leigh: undertaker
Thomas Hutchinson: lieutenant governor of the Massachusetts colony
Townspeople
Children
Other British Soldiers
Note: All townspeople's and children's parts can be played by one group of actors.

SETTING

A customs house. A sentry stands guard on a winter day. He paces back and forth. People are walking by.

(Father, son, and daughter stop before customs house. Children pick up some stones and try to hit the pacing sentry.)

Townsperson #1: Looks like the children have found themselves a new game.

(Some people stop to watch and laugh. The sentry charges forward a few steps. The family moves on hurriedly.)

Townsperson #2: I'd like to burn down that customs house, but not before taking the money they've robbed me of.

Townsperson #3: Yes, burning the customs house would take the chill out of the cold March wind.

(A man in a cloak ENTERS, carrying broadsides.)

Cloaked Man *(gathering people around him)*: Redcoats are going to attack us! That's right! Attack us. (More people stop.) Remember the dockman who hit the soldier? Well, the soldier told his redcoat friends. Look, look! Notices signed by the redcoats. They promise to attack us. (The cloaked man hands out some broadsides and then EXITS. Narrator steps out of the crowd.)

Narrator: This is Boston in 1770. Not a calm place. Colonists and British soldiers are constantly mistreating each other. Colonists complain about unfair laws passed by the king. The soldiers walk around frightening colonists in hope of cooling their protests. See for yourself.

(A British soldier ENTERS.)

Samuel Grey *(steps forward from crowd of people chatting)*: Hey, Lobsterback, come here.

Soldier #1: I don't answer to such names.

Samuel Grey: I beg your pardon. I didn't know you would let a name get between you and a chance to earn some money. (The soldier comes closer.) I want to know if you are looking for work.

Soldier #1: I am, faith.

Samuel Grey: Well, good. You can clean out my outhouse. (The crowd laughs.)

(The soldier swings at Grey. Grey's friends come to his assistance. They knock the soldier down. A sword falls from the soldier. They pick it up and chase the soldier off. The soldier EXITS. He ENTERS with more soldiers. A shoving match begins, but it is stopped by John Grey, owner of a ropeworks.)

John Grey: All right, Samuel, that is enough. Your hands should be for ropemaking, not fighting.

(The soldiers, Samuel Grey, and his friends circulate among the crowd. The crowd calls the soldiers names: devils, lobsterbacks, villains. The British soldiers shove people around. A group of colonists gathers in front of the action. The soldiers and the crowd cease their bickering and EXIT. Four townspeople remain.)

Townsperson #1: Redcoats whacking colonists. Colonists whacking redcoats. Bad times.

Townsperson #2: It's that wicked Townshend Act. That is the cause of people's anger. Putting a tax on English paper, lead, glass, paint, and tea. What's left?

Townsperson #3: We can do without their goods.

Townsperson #1: I suppose, but I don't like the coffee my wife's been giving me. I'm a tea drinker.

Townsperson #4: It's not the tax that bothers me. It's what the Parliament does with the money they collect. They pay our officials, *our* elected officials. That's what bothers me. We are supposed to pay them. If the Parliament pays them, why should these officials listen to us?

Townsperson #3: Yes. Why should they indeed? (The townspeople EXIT. A boy ENTERS. He steps up to the sentry and throws a rock at him.)

Sentry: Ouch! Why you . . .

(Sentry hits him with the butt of his rifle. Boy EXITS in tears. Narrator ENTERS.)

Narrator: The boy leaves to tell his father the sentry hit him. The father tells his friends. Soon most of Boston knows what has happened. Everyone agrees the sentry has to be taught a lesson.

(Church bells are ringing in the background. A crowd ENTERS. The people gather around the customs house, waving sticks.)

COSTUMES

Actors Who Are Not Playing British Soldiers

White, gray, or brown shirts; long pants, not jeans; light-colored or white knee-length socks (stuff the pants into the socks); brown or black shoes, no sneakers; a cloak for the CLOAKED MAN.

Actors Who Are Playing British Soldiers

White shirt, red coat or sweater, white pants, long white socks, black or brown shoes, two belts to be wrapped in crisscross fashion across jacket.

All Girls

Long simple dress, mop cap or bonnet, plain shoes (no sneakers or high heels), large square scarf to be worn around the shoulders and crisscrossed in the front and tucked into the waistband of the dress.

PROPS

Muskets: long cardboard tubes (or short tubes taped together). Cut a triangular piece of cardboard. Make two slits on either side of the triangle and wedge the piece onto the edge of the cardboard tube.
Sticks
Styrofoam balls for the *snowballs*
Pieces of unlined paper
Crumpled paper bags (small) for *rocks*
Swords
Sound effect: hand claps for sound of gun shots.

Crispus Attucks fell dead.

Townsperson #3 *(pointing to the sentry)*: That's the beast that hit the boy with his gun.

(The crowd throws rocks and snowballs at the sentry. Soldiers begin coming out and gather around the customs house.)

British Officer: Men, return to your barracks.

Crowd: Knock them down! Kill them! Kill them!

(Sticks are waved. British reinforcements ENTER with their captain, Captain Preston.)

Soldiers *(pushing through the crowd)*: Make way!

Crowd: Don't push. Get that sword away.

Captain Preston *(standing in front of his troops, speaks to the crowd)*: I ask you all to leave this place. If someone has been wronged, I will speak to that person.

Crowd: We have all been wronged!

(Crispus Attucks, a runaway slave, steps forward from the crowd, away from Captain Preston.)

Crispus Attucks: Kill the dogs! Knock them down!

(He grabs a soldier's gun. The soldier grabs onto the gun. Attucks tries to wrestle the gun away. The captain notices the scuffle. Actors freeze as Narrator steps forward.)

Narrator: Who is this man who acts so boldly? He is Crispus Attucks, a runaway slave. Some colonists call him a troublemaker. Others call him a daring rebel. Either way, he would be the first African American to die for the colonies' independence. He would not be the last.

(The action begins again.)

Townsperson #3: Sir, I hope you don't intend the soldiers shall fire on the colonists?

Captain Preston: By no means. (Preston turns to the soldier fighting with Attucks.) Soldier, stop . . .

(The soldier manages to get his gun back. He fires upon Attucks. Attucks falls dead. A snowball strikes a soldier standing next to the captain. The soldier steps forward and fires his gun. Other soldiers fire their guns. Nine more shots are fired in all. The crowd steps back to reveal five dead men. Seven are wounded. Benjamin Leigh, the undertaker, steps forward to Captain Preston.)

Leigh: Captain. (The captain stands in a daze.) Captain Preston.

Captain Preston: Yes, Sir.

Leigh: I will try to calm these people. I advise you to detach your men. (To the crowd) Please calm yourselves. Let the dead and wounded be taken care of.

(The captain withdraws his men. More people gather. They yell for justice. They chant, "Murderers." Lieutenant Governor Thomas Hutchinson ENTERS. He stands in front of the customs house.)

Hutchinson: Ladies and gentlemen.

(The crowd boos him. They call him a villain. They call for justice.)

Hutchinson: Ladies and gentlemen. Your cries for justice have not fallen upon deaf ears. Justice will be done. Let British law take its course. I ask you to retire. (They do not retire.)

Leigh: Please leave and let the dead and wounded be attended to. (The crowd slowly retires, taking the dead and wounded with them. Narrator is left on stage.)

Narrator: The Boston Massacre could have been avoided. Five people's lives could have been spared. Today, March 5, 1770, on the very day of this bloody massacre, the Parliament repealed the evil Townshend Act, which surely caused this violence. But the news had to come by ship. The colonists would not know the Townshend Act had been repealed till many days later.

OCTOBER 5, 1772: Adams Calls for Committees of Correspondence. At a special Boston town meeting, Sam Adams called upon citizens in every town to organize "committees of correspondence." Adams wants emergency networks to watch and report local British activities to members in other colonial towns.

A BITTER BREW

Tea is a beverage made from leaves steeped in boiling water. This simple drink satisfied many colonists when they were cold, tired, or both.

British tea, however, was not so simple a brew. It had one ingredient besides tea leaves and water. A tax. This tax added bitterness to the drink.

The tax, however, was small enough that many colonists didn't bother to challenge it. In fact, many colonists didn't bother to challenge anything between 1770 and 1773. They were more interested in making money. This attitude worried Samuel Adams. At this rate, there would be no revolution.

The Parliament came to Adams's rescue, though they didn't intend to, by passing the Tea Act of 1773. It was a law the colonists were certain to hate.

The Tea Act gave the East India Company, a British trading company, the right to determine who could sell tea in the colonies.

The colonists understood what that meant. Anyone loyal to the king could sell tea. Anyone who protested against the king would have to find something else to sell.

Tea sellers were furious. All colonial merchants were scared. If Parliament could control who sold tea, they could control who sold anything in the colonies.

The Tea Act of 1773 woke up the sleeping colonists. Those rebels who wanted to be free of the king once again had the attention of everyone.

DECEMBER 16, 1773: Shipment of Tea Dumped into Boston Harbor. Partly in protest over tea tax, angry patriots boarded three British ships in Boston Harbor tonight. Hacking open 342 wooden crates and throwing them overboard, they destroyed the entire cargo of imported Indian tea.

Tea Facts

One million colonists drank tea twice a day. Some of that tea was smuggled into the colonies.

In England, where there was also a tea tax, over six million pounds of tea were smuggled into the country every year!

Grandfather Peck's Tea Party

"We raised our hatchets and smashed open the chests."

"It began with a meeting . . ."

"No, grandfather," pleaded Samuel Peck's grandson, "start the story with you putting the paint on your face."

"As you wish. It was the night of December 16, 1773, when John Peters, Anthony Morse, Thomas Moore, and I tiptoed through the street to the Edes and Gills printing office and up the stairs to the 'long room.' That was our secret meeting place for the 'Long Room Club.' It was there Samuel Adams, and the rest of us—his rabble-rousing Sons of Liberty—thought up the idea to dress as Indians and dump the British tea into the harbor.

"We opened cans of paint and colored our faces copper. We put on Indian feathered headdresses, and covered ourselves in buckskin and blankets. Over at the Green Dragon Tavern, and at John Crane's house, other men were doing the same. Soon it was time to go. We gathered axes and pistols and left to join the others at Hollis and Tremont streets. What a sight we were. An Indian village, that's what we looked like.

"We walked, quietly, down to the wharf. On the way, we stopped at the Old South Meeting House.

"The meeting house was packed. There were crowds of people all around listening to Samuel Adams talk about what to do with the tea sitting on the ships in Boston Harbor. The door was wide open so the people on the porch could hear. John Rowe, a friend of Adams, suggested what he thought should be done with the tea.

"'Who knows,' said John Rowe, 'how tea will mingle with salt water?'

"The people inside and on the porch cried out with approval. 'A mob! A mob!' they shouted. Then Samuel Adams said, 'This meeting can do nothing more to save the country.'

"That was our signal. We let out the loudest, most piercing howl we could muster. That got everyone's attention.

"'The Mohawks come!' shouted a man inside the meeting hall. 'Boston Harbor a tea-pot tonight.'

"The meeting ended right there and then. The crowds followed us to the wharf. When we got there I warned the customs officer, 'If you keep your own way peaceably, we shall keep ours.'

"The officer stood aside. And we boarded the *Dartmouth*. Others boarded the *Eleanor* and the *Beaver* and began hoisting up tea chests from ships' bellies.

"We wasted no time. There in the moonlight, we raised our hatchets and smashed open the chests. Wood splinters flew. We dumped the tea overboard into the harbor below. Even in the darkness you could see the tea leaves stain the water a deep brown.

"And when the last chest of tea was thrown overboard, we swept the ships' decks clean and went home.

"The next day I said nothing at the cooperage [a barrelmaking shop] where I worked. It would have been foolish to boast about dumping the tea into the harbor. I could have been arrested.

"So I kept my mouth shut. I began instructing my ten-year-old apprentices on the fine points of banding the wood staves together to form a barrel. But the boys would not pay attention. All they did was giggle and whisper to each other. We got nothing done that day.

"That night I told my wife about the apprentices and she broke into laughter herself.

"'Samuel,' she scolded me with a big smile, 'how many times have I told you to wash behind your ears? The backs of your ears are covered in copper paint for the whole world to see.'

"'So that's what the boys were laughing about.' I immediately got up to wash the paint off.

"I was lucky. I might have been arrested. So, listen to me. If you remember anything about this story, grandson, remember always to wash behind your ears."

Did You Know?

That night, at the Boston Tea Party, on December 16, 1773, 342 chests of tea worth approximately $6,000 were dumped overboard into Boston Harbor. Today the same amount of tea would be worth over $17,000.

We Will Survive

Samuel Adams was not about to let the closing of Boston Harbor frighten him. He said, "Our oppressors cannot force us into submission by reducing us to a state of starvation. We can exist independently of all the world. The real wants and necessities of man are few. Nature has bountifully supplied us with the means of nourishment; and if all fail, we can, like our ancestors, live on the clams and mussels which abound on our shore."

THE KING PUNISHES BOSTON

When a door is closed strangers are kept out. When a window is closed the wind is kept out. When a port is closed a way of life is kept out.

In late spring of 1774 British ships formed a blockade around the port of Boston. All sea trade was to stop. No ship could leave. No ship could enter. Even simple fishing boats were not permitted. The people of Boston relied on their port. Trade with ships provided many of the goods necessary for survival.

The blockade was Boston's punishment for dumping 342 chests of tea into Boston Harbor. The port would be reopened only after the dumped tea was paid for and the people showed a willingness to be loyal to the king.

Boston is surrounded by water on three sides. Only a narrow strip of land provided a link between the city and the mainland. At high tide this strip of land was almost completely covered with water.

Boston was at the mercy of British warships and the king. Would Parliament and the king be merciful? The citizens were doubtful. It seemed clear that the intention of Parliament and the king was to starve the people of Boston.

News of Boston's situation traveled fast. The colonists responded immediately. Donations of money, corn, rye, rice, and dried fish were sent by wagon. New York sent a flock of sheep and this guarantee: "We will supply you with enough food to last out a siege of ten years."

Food, however, was not Boston's only concern. The Boston Port Bill, which closed Boston Harbor, was one in a series of three acts designed to teach the city a lesson. The acts created hunger, denied colonists the right to elect their own officials, and prohibited public meetings. The colonists called them the "Intolerable Acts." To the king and his minister, Lord North, the acts were sweet revenge. Lord North threatened, "The colonies must either submit or triumph."

SEPTEMBER 5, 1774: First Continental Congress Meets in Philadelphia. Fifty-six representatives of twelve colonies met at Carpenters' Hall in Philadelphia to discuss British abuses. Georgia refused to attend. Delegates elected Peyton Randolph of Virginia as president and pledged discussions to secrecy.

THE FIRST CONTINENTAL CONGRESS

It was clear that a new way of governing had to be created—a government that represented the colonists, not the king.

In Virginia the assembly boldly stated, "A Congress should be appointed . . . from all the colonies to concert [make] a general and uniform plan for defense and preservation of our common rights. . . ."

This congress, called the Continental Congress, was to be held in Philadelphia. Here, citizens believed in the rights of colonists, as well as in ending slavery.

To this town merchants and craftsmen, Quakers and Catholics, southerners and northerners arrived to a church-bell welcome.

From the opening day of the congress on September 1, 1774, to the final day on October 26, delegates argued. They argued over where the congress should be held, whether larger colonies should have more votes than smaller colonies. In committees, farmers argued with merchants. Rebellious delegates lost their patience with delegates seeking to find a compromise with the king.

In the end, however, the reading of the Suffolk Resolve united the delegates to denounce the Intolerable Acts and force all colonists to stop buying British goods.

ADAMS'S NEW CLOTHES

The tempting smell of fish chowder and fresh-baked bread drifted through Samuel Adams's house. In his library, Adams stopped reading to take notice of his wife's preparations. He would miss her cooking while he was away.

Adams thought about his journey next week to the First Continental Congress in Philadelphia. It would be hard on his health and his finances. Sitting in a carriage and sleeping in strange beds for over two weeks would worsen Adams's arthritis.

It was also a trip he couldn't afford. His son, a doctor, and the community were paying for his travel expenses. Still, Adams had no money to replace his worn clothing. This didn't bother him. He cared little about clothes.

What he cared about most was participating in this congress in Philadelphia. This wasn't the first congress. Nine years earlier, in 1765, there had been the Stamp Act Congress to protest the unfair Stamp Act, but only nine of the thirteen colonies attended. This First Continental Congress promised to have twelve of the thirteen colonies in attendance. Here was the greatest opportunity to produce a united stand for independence.

Elizabeth, Adams's wife, called the family to the dinner table. Adams left his study and joined his family. There was a knock on the door.

"Who could that be?" asked Elizabeth, annoyed by the interruption. "Are you expecting someone, Samuel?"

"No," he replied, getting up.

At the door was Boston's finest tailor.

"Can I help you?" asked Adams.

"Yes," said the tailor, stepping inside. "I need to take some measurements."

"There must be some mistake. I did not call you here," Adams said in a stern voice.

"I did not say you did," said the tailor. "There. I am finished. I apologize for the disturbance. A good evening to you and your family."

Adams returned to the dinner table. There was another knock on the door. It was a shirtmaker. He too would not say who had sent him. The shirtmaker was followed by the haberdasher [hat maker], and the shoemaker. When Adams finally returned to his meal it was cold, but he wasn't hungry. He was distracted by the question: Who is having new clothes made for me?

The day before he was to depart for Philadelphia, Adams found a trunk outside his front door. Inside were two complete suits of clothes, two new pairs of shoes with silver buckles, a set of gold knee buckles and another of gold sleeve buttons, a deep red cloak, a cocked hat, and a gold-headed cane.

Adams examined the clothing. He was pleased to find the fabric had been made in the colonies. Adams started to close the trunk when he noticed something on the cane that looked familiar. He picked it up. Imprinted on the cane's head was a Sons of Liberty emblem. Samuel Adams now knew who had paid for his new clothes.

A TIRELESS MESSENGER FOR THE SONS OF LIBERTY

Paul Revere had one thought on his mind: the Continental Congress must see the Suffolk Resolve. This document captured the daring spirit that all colonists should hold.

He placed the paper in his saddlebag and rode out of Milton, Massachusetts, bound for Philadelphia, Pennsylvania.

It was a ten-day ride. The dirt roads were pocked with holes. At times the roads were blocked by farmers moving their sheep from one field to another. Revere was ready. He had traveled the road many times, delivering messages for the Sons of Liberty. He was known by the colonists to "give you all the news." When an important event happened in Massachusetts, people knew Revere was riding down the Post Road to New York, or heading to Pennsylvania. Revere was a tireless messenger for the Sons of Liberty. He was also the fastest. Paul Revere arrived in Philadelphia in seven days, setting a new record! This didn't please him half as much as seeing the congress cheering and shouting when the Suffolk Resolve was read to them.

Telling It Like It Is

The delegates from Suffolk County, Massachusetts, didn't hide their anger over the coercive or Intolerable Acts passed by Parliament and the king.

The Suffolk Resolve stated that these acts were "the attempts of a wicked administration to enslave America."

The delegates believed that the Parliament was taking away rights their ancestors had fought for. They also believed that any official paid by the king, instead of the colonists, should resign. Those that did not were enemies of the colonies.

Finally, the delegates ordered that a town militia be organized and seize anyone who served "the present tyrannical and unconstitutional government."

Paul Revere, the tireless messenger for the Sons of Liberty.

Spy Stories

The horses began to get restless.

Paul Revere's Thieves

Paul Revere called his spy group the "mechanics." The word *mechanic* means someone who works with their hands.

Revere started the mechanics spy ring for people who worked with their hands because the Sons of Liberty, the most popular secret club in Boston, was a club for businessmen.

In December of 1774, the mechanics learned two British regiments were taking a hundred kegs of gunpowder to be stored in Portsmouth, New Hampshire. The regiments crossed the river and marched north. They did not get much farther.

Revere's men surprised the British regiments. Several soldiers fired their guns, but the mechanics quickly surrounded the British and put and end to their resistance. The hundred kegs of gunpowder became rebel property and were later used at the Battle of Breed's Hill.

"Stop," the British soldier ordered the wagon driver.

The driver knew what the sentry wanted: to look in his wagon for hidden guns. The driver had guns. They were inside the barrels of flour he was transporting.

"Where are you coming from?"

"Concord," said the man in the wagon.

"What are you carrying?"

"I'm carrying what I always carry," the man replied, looking straight into the soldier's face.

"What is that?"

"Flour. Barrels of flour," replied the man.

"I'll take a look if you don't mind."

"Look all you want," dared the man in the wagon. "I'm loyal to our king."

Searching wagons was commonplace. Throughout the Massachusetts Bay Colony, rebels were preparing to defend themselves. Rebel colonists thought about nothing else but storing weapons and food—not for winter, but for war.

Kitchens became bullet factories. Fireplaces became foundries, melting down anything made of lead and recasting the soft metal into bullets. Countryside barns were becoming gun factories.

The sentry began prying open a barrel. Not far away, boys played marbles and watched. The driver winked at a boy. The boy signaled to a woman looking out her window. The woman came outside and started shooing her chickens around to the wagon. The man nudged his horses. The horses began to get restless.

"Come here, chick, chick. Come here," said the woman.

"Hold your horses," commanded the soldier. "Get those chickens away," he yelled to the woman.

"I can't hold them much longer," said the wagon driver. "My horses can't stand chickens," he stated, nudging his horses once more.

"Get those . . ."

The soldier did not finish his sentence. The wagon began to roll. The soldier raised his gun. He lowered it in frustration. He knew firing his gun would surely cause a riot. Boston was a powder keg ready to explode. It was also a city teeming with spies.

Secrets at the Green Dragon Tavern

"Do you swear by almighty God that what is said here will be repeated to no one?"

"We do," said the men seated at the tables.

And so began another meeting of the spy network called the "mechanics." Organized by Paul Revere, the mechanics spent their days watching every move British soldiers made.

"First," said Paul Revere with a smile, "a moment of silence for the British cannon that accidentally fell to the bottom of Mill Pond the other night."

The men listening roared with laughter and took large sips of molasses and rum.

"All right, boys, what have you heard?" said Revere.

A man with a broad smile on his face stated, "There's a lot more cannon that need to be given their first and last swimming lesson in Mill Pond."

"Take care of it—quietly," advised Revere. His smile was gone.

Lately, the British seemed to know about the mechanics' secret activities. How could they know? Paul Revere searched the faces of his friends, but said nothing. Someone in this room was a British spy, but who?

In the Countryside

John Howe was a skilled gunsmith. He was also a British spy under orders from British General Thomas Gage. Howe was to appear as a traveler and determine the strength of the rebel militia in each town he passed, the size of its munitions supplies, and the number of arms factories.

Howe had just finished dinner served by his host, the loyalist Squire Barnes. He sat down with the journal in which he kept notes on what he had seen since he left Boston three days ago.

John Howe was nervous. If he were caught with these papers, he knew it would be tar and feathers for him, perhaps even death on the gallows. John Howe began to write in his journal the number of militiamen he saw training today in Marlboro.

There was a knock at the front door. Six rebel colonists stood at the loyalist Squire's doorstep.

A voice said, "Squire Barnes, we have come to search your house for spies."

"I am willing," replied Barnes.

John Howe closed his journal and collected his papers. He raced upstairs, climbed out a window, and slid onto the snow-covered roof. He stepped forward and fell, sliding off the roof and onto the ground. He ran into the frozen swamp. In the distance he saw the light of another house. He ran with all his might. He knocked on the door and prayed that he would be let in.

A black man opened the door. He looked suspiciously at Howe. There was no reason for a man to be out at this time of night, unless he was a British spy looking for a place to hide.

"Evening, Sir," said Howe.

"Awful late to be knocking on a stranger's door," commented the man.

"That is true, but I am dead tired. I'm on my way to Concord to . . . ," John Howe leaned in and whispered, "make guns to use against the British troops."

"You should have planned better so you didn't have to look for shelter so late at night," scolded the man. "But you are welcome to sleep here."

"Thank you for your kindness," said Howe.

The next day the man took Howe by boat across the Concord River. Because Howe was a skillful gunsmith, he was introduced to Major Buttrick in Concord. The major asked Howe to repair militia guns. Howe spent the day.

Trusting this new gunsmith, the major showed Howe the town's hidden weapons and munitions. This new information would be the last entry in Howe's journal. The next day he presented his journal to General Gage in Boston.

Coffee, Tea, or Trouble?

When John Howe walked into a tavern filled with rebel patriots, he would order a glass of molasses and rum or a cup of coffee. These drinks were passwords strangers used to tell other patriots they were opposed to King George III.

However, in a tavern loyal to the king, the owner would come up to British spy Howe and say quietly, "Have what you please, either tea or coffee." This told him that if he was loyal to the king he was among friends.

Still, if a British spy didn't know much about the tavern he walked into, he could be tricked. The owner, a rebel, could ask if he wanted coffee or tea to test him.

He ran with all his might.

A Secret Message

General Gage was pleased with Howe's work, but not by what he read in Howe's journal. It was obvious that the rebels were preparing for war. General Gage did not want to attack the militia, for that would surely start the war. He decided destroying the rebels' supplies was the safest course of action. The question was: When to act?

April 9, 1775. A messenger, sent by a British spy in Concord, rushed into General Gage's office. His cheeks were flushed, and he was short of breath.

"This is from Concord," declared the messenger, trying to remain calm.

The British officer took the letter and broke the wax seal. He brushed the letter with a special solution always at hand. Suddenly, new words appeared between the lines: *"Strike at once!"*

The British officer brought the message to General Gage, who called his most trusted officers. Gage told them, "You will pick your best eight hundred troops. They will leave Boston on April 18, at night. The troops will cross the Charles River and march to Lexington. They will reach Lexington at dawn. By arriving early,

you will be sure no rebel is awake to disturb your men. Using information provided to us by loyal spies, your troops are to find the hidden supplies and destroy them, then march to Concord and do the same before returning home. Need I remind you that your preparations are to be made in utmost secrecy?"

Secrets could not be kept from the mechanics. Lexington and Concord were warned. Hidden weapons and food were moved to new locations. British spies were watching the rebels. They sent letters of warning to British headquarters in Boston, but would they arrive in time?

A Night of Warnings

On the night of April 18, the mechanics waited to see which way the British troops would travel to Lexington and Concord. There were two choices. They could travel by land or cross the Charles River. Once the mechanics knew which route the troops were taking, the countryside could be warned.

The British troops had no idea they were being watched.

Said Doctor Belknap, "On the night of April 18, they [British troops] took every imaginable precaution to prevent a discovery. . . . They were waked up by the sergeants putting their hands on them, and whispering gently to them. . . .

"They walked through the streets with the utmost silence. A dog, happening to bark, was instantly killed with a bayonet. . . . They proceeded to the beach under the new powderhouse, the most unfrequented part of town; and

They would cross the river.

there embarked on board the boats which had their oars muffled to prevent a noise."

The troops would cross the river. Paul Revere and William Dawes were on their way to warn the countryside. They took different paths, but would meet in Lexington.

Revere and Dawes rode in the shadows, throwing pebbles at windows and shouting that British troops were coming. Each warning betrayed the king's troops. Their ride to Lexington was an act of treason.

Revere and Dawes met in Lexington. Together they started to Concord with Doctor Prescott, whom they met traveling on the same road. On the way they met a British patrol. Dawes and Prescott escaped. Revere was captured. After being questioned, he was released, but the patrol kept his horse. Revere continued to warn the countryside on foot.

DOCTOR SPY

Paul Revere was right. There *was* a spy among the mechanics. Could it be Doctor Church, the patriot?

General Washington had no doubt about it, nor did the baker who brought his story of Church's treacherous deeds to Washington's attention.

The baker told Washington that a woman named Lisa had asked him if he knew any British officers. He did know a British naval officer. Lisa asked him to deliver a letter to this officer. The baker agreed.

The baker wondered why Lisa was so determined that he deliver a message to this British officer. He became curious. He opened the letter.

Inside, he found words that made no sense to him. It looked like the letters in each word had been mixed up.

> ZXXVKG ML HFY-
> HGRGFGY ULI UFM!!

The baker realized the letter was written in code.

He gave the peculiar letter to Washington. The general ordered the woman found and brought to him.

Lisa stood before General Washington. "Who gave you this letter?" questioned Washington.

"Is that my letter?" she answered innocently.

"Don't deny it! I have talked to the baker."

"I have nothing to say," stated Lisa.

"Nothing but a full confession can save you from hanging," warned the general.

Lisa's confident voice faded after an hour. After two hours she was trembling, but refused to reveal who gave her the coded letter. All night Lisa heard the same question over and over: "Who gave you this letter?"

Finally, on the edge of collapse, she said, "Doctor Benjamin Church, Jr."

Doctor Church was arrested. Three men went to work to break the coded letter. The code was broken. The letter contained a report on the colonies' ability to fight a war. There was information on the strength of the colonial militia and on the amount of munitions and food.

Doctor Church's Code

Here is what Doctor Church wrote about the congress in Philadelphia. Can you break the code?

"Fmrgvw, wvgvinrmvw rm lkklhrgrlm."

Hint: In this code A = Z, B = Y, C = X, and so on. Now make your own code and send messages to your friends.

Paul Revere rode in the shadows.

British Spy: A Board Game

Object of the game: You are a British spy. Your mission is to gather information about the rebels: How many soldiers they have, how many guns, and how much food they have hidden. Can you accomplish your mission and make it back to your leader, General Gage, in Boston? Or will you get caught?

What You Need:

One die; three quarter-size cardboard circles that are colored red, white, and blue; one or two other players.

Each British spy rolls the die. The person who rolls the highest number starts first. The person who rolls the second highest starts second. The other spy starts last.

The first spy rolls the die. Whatever number the die shows, move your colored marker that many spaces around the board. Follow the instructions of whatever space you land on.

The first spy to return to Boston with the information for British general Gage wins.

Note: A player must roll the exact number to reach Boston and win.

BOSTON:

Space 1: Your wagon breaks down.

Space 2: Hidden boat takes you across the river to Charlestown. *Move ahead two spaces.*

Space 3: General Gage gives orders for you to have his fastest horse. *Move ahead two spaces.*

CHARLESTOWN:

Space 4: Rebel colonist tells you about munitions supplies hidden nearby.

Space 5: Thirsty; stop at tavern for a drink.

Space 6: British officer at tavern tells you to stay overnight for your own safety. *Lose one turn.*

WATERTOWN:

Space 7: Stop at Jonathan Brewer's Tavern. Given ride to Framingham. Learn about arms factory in Framingham. *Move ahead six spaces.*

Space 8: Anxious to continue. Decide not to stop overnight.

Space 9: Black maid at Jonathan Brewer's Tavern recognizes you. Rebels tar and feather you. Return to Boston to recover and start over again. *Go back to start.*

WESTON:

Space 10: Accidentally order tea at rebel tavern. Joel Smith throws you out. *Move back two spaces.*

Space 11: Loyalist Captain Jones has friend show you hidden rebel food supplies.

Space 12: It's raining. Stay put.

FRAMINGHAM:

Space 13: See arms factory. Noticed by rebel who was at Weston Tavern.

Space 14: Rest at stranger's house and update journal in secret.

Space 15: Your lucky day. Given a ride to Worcester. *Move ahead four spaces.*

MARLBORO:

Space 16: Squire Barnes gives you breakfast. His friend takes you to see rebels drill.

Space 17: Rebels chase you from Squire Barnes's home. You fall and sprain your ankle in a ditch. Must rest. *Lose one turn.*

Space 18: Fellow British spy tells you Gage wants you in Concord. *Move ahead two spaces.*

WORCESTER:

Space 19: Among friends loyal to the king. Decide to stay.

Space 20: Drop spy journal on the road somewhere between Worcester and Framingham. *Move back four spaces.*

Space 21: Nothing to see in Worcester. *Move ahead one space.*

CONCORD:

Space 22: Meet with fellow British spy Daniel Bliss. Taken to see nearby guns factory outside of town.

Space 23: Rebels find you at the home of British spy Major Thompson. Run for your life! *Move back four spaces.*

Space 24: You have all the information you need. *Roll a one and you're home free in Boston.*

BOSTON:

Give your journal to General Gage. Sit down and relax!

Secret Messages

Spies were very concerned about keeping their messages as secret as possible. Messages were written in invisible ink, even in a foreign language. Some spies simply left out letters in a word to make it difficult to read.

Here are some coded messages. You decide if the messages are true or false:

D-ct-r C-urch w-s a h-ro.

Brit-sh spie- -n B-st-n r-port-d -o G-ner-l G-ge.

T-e m-chan-cs f-xed w-g-ns.

N- militiam-n w-re k-lle- i- L-xingt-n.

S-ies us-d inv-sibl- i-k.

J-hn How- wa- a reb-l s-y.

P-triots dran- t-a.

Charlest-wn and B-sto- a-e -n th- s-me s-de -f t-e r-ver.

One If By Land, Two If By Water

On April 16, Paul Revere made his way to Lexington to warn two patriots, Samuel Adams and John Hancock, that the British were planning to march on Concord in two days. On his way back he stopped in Charlestown to talk to his friend Colonel Conant.

Revere told Colonel Conant that on the night of April 18 he must watch the Christ Church Steeple in Boston.

Someone would signal him by lantern. The person would wave one lantern if the British troops were traveling by land, two if the troops were crossing over the Charles River.

Revere and his friend Dawes planned to warn the Massachusetts countryside themselves, but just in case they were stopped by British troops, Conant would still be able to spread the news that the British were coming.

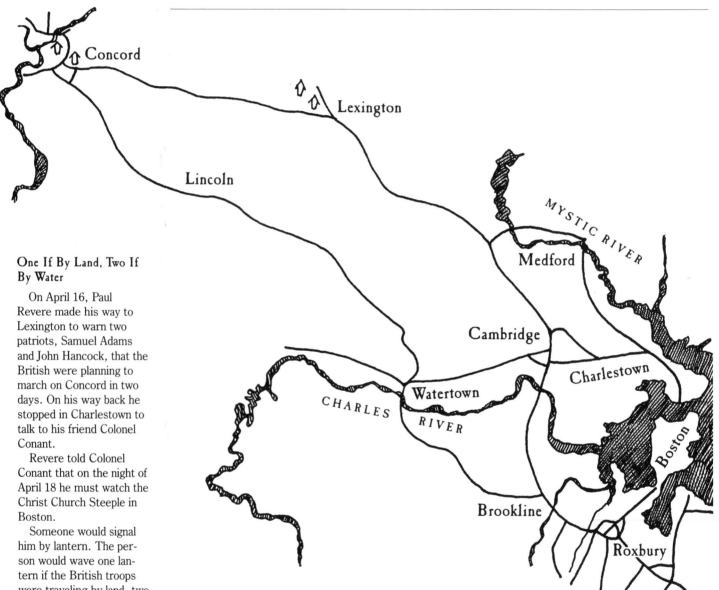

Boston, Lexington, and Concord, 1775

This colonial political cartoon shows the British retreating from Lexington. If you look carefully, you can see that all the British soldiers have donkey heads!

The First Battles

The eight hundred British troops marched all night. They were tired. They wanted to destroy the rebel supplies in Lexington and Concord and get home.

It would not be that simple. When the sun appeared on April 19, bells rang out alerting the people that British troops were entering Lexington. Major Pitcairn's British regiment approached the green where the militia was waiting.

"Ye villains, ye rebels, disperse!" came shouts from the British, who were frustrated to find rebels waiting for them. "Lay down your arms!"

The colonial militia was outnumbered. It began to withdraw, but they did not lay down their arms.

A shot rang out from the British ranks. Then more shots were fired.

Major Pitcairn screamed at his men to cease firing. They did, but it was too late. Eight rebels lay dead, shot in the back. Nine more were wounded.

The British marched to Concord. They searched for the militia's supplies, but they did not know where to look. The supplies had been moved, and the British spy letters revealing the new hiding places had not reached Boston in time.

Several muskets were found and burned. Barrels of flour were tossed in the water.

To make up for this empty victory, a redcoat patrol attempted to secure North Bridge, which crossed the Concord River. Militiamen were sit-uated atop a hill across from the bridge. They spotted smoke rising from trees in front of Concord. The militiamen incorrectly thought the British had set Concord on fire and charged down the hill. The British fired. The militiamen returned fire and killed three redcoats.

The battle lasted just several minutes, but it would be remembered forever. It was the first battle of the Revolutionary War.

With few officers among the British patrol, the soldiers retreated back into town and began the march back to Boston. The troops had destroyed whatever rebel supplies they could. Their work was done.

But it was not over. Rebel forces descended upon Concord. They were in the woods, at Meriam's Corner, waiting for the troops to leave town.

British troops were marching down the road, in the open. The rebels opened fire. Women fired at the British from nearby houses. The British troops were confused. They were not trained to fight a hidden enemy, only an enemy that faced them in an open field.

British troops marched on to Boston as the stream of bullets cut them down. Some soldiers rushed into nearby rebel houses seeking revenge. They set houses on fire, stole valuables, and killed citizens.

Seventy-three redcoats were killed, and 174 were wounded before British reinforcements arrived. An open field was covered with British bodies.

The Revolutionary War had begun.

They were ambushed and a great many were killed.

The War Begins

Amos Barrett was a twenty-three-year-old minuteman. He took part in the Battle of Concord and the ambush of British troops. This is his story:

We marched into town [Concord] . . . and then over the North Bridge and then on a hill not far from the bridge. . . . Eighty or ninety British came to the bridge and there made a halt. After awhile they begun to tear up the plank of the bridge. Major Buttrick said if we were all of his mind, he would drive them away from the bridge. We all said we would go.

We then marched on . . . they fired on us— their balls whistled well. We then was all ordered to fire that could fire and not kill our own men. It is strange that warn't no more killed, but they fired too high.

We soon drove them from the bridge. When I got there was two lay dead and another almost

dead. We did not follow after them. There was eight or ten that was wounded, and a-running and hobbling about, looking back to see if we was after them. . . .

We then saw the whole body a-coming out of town. We then was ordered to lay behind the wall. Major Buttrick said he would give the word "fire." The Commanding [British] officer ordered the whole battalion to halt. . . . There we lay behind the wall, about two hundred of us with our guns cocked, expecting every minute to have the word "fire." But we had no orders to fire. . . . They stayed about ten minutes and then marched back.

After a while we found them a-marching back towards Boston. . . . We was soon after them . . . they was ambushed and a great many killed. When I got there, a great many lay dead and the road was bloody.

Joseph Palmer's Alarm

He took a deep breath and wrote the most important letter of his life.

Committees of Correspondence

Every town in every colony had a Committee of Correspondence. Each committee was like a person in a relay race. If something important happened in one town, a letter was written and sent by horseback or ship to the next committee. This committee, in turn, sent it on to the next, until every committee in every town in every colony had been informed.

In 1774, with the fear of war between the colonies and Britain, the Committees of Correspondence became known as the Committees of Safety.

The Battles of Lexington and Concord were fought on April 19, 1775. British troops fired upon militiamen at Lexington. Militiamen fired upon British soldier at Concord. It was the start of the Revolutionary War.

The *Massachusetts Spy* printed its first story about the Battles of Lexington and Concord on May 3:

"AMERICANS! forever bear in mind the BATTLE OF LEXINGTON!—where British Troops, without cause, viciously and in a most inhuman manner fired upon and killed a number of our countrymen. . . ."

But how did the *Spy* get the information to write its story about the battle? There were no telephones. There were no television reporters at Lexington and Concord to report on the battle as it happened.

Townspeople were the first to pass on the news. They raced to their neighbors to spread the word that militiamen had been killed. The first neighbors to be notified were the members of the Lexington Committee of Correspondence, whose job it was to pass on important news.

The Lexington committee hurriedly drafted a note. Isaac Bissel was standing by his horse, waiting. When the note was completed, he thrust it into his leather pouch and tossed the pouch over his shoulder. Isaac mounted his horse and raced to Watertown, eight miles away.

He arrived a half-hour later and knocked at the door of Joseph Palmer, the head of the Committee of Correspondence in Watertown. Joseph Palmer opened the door.

"What have you got?" asked Palmer.

"A note from Lexington. British troops killed eight men and wounded nine others."

"Let me see it," said Palmer anxiously. "My

God," said Palmer, scanning the note. "The war has finally begun." Palmer turned to Bissel. "I have to rewrite this note before passing it on."

"I'll wait here," said Bissel.

"No. Go get Silas Deane. I'll need a witness to sign this letter as well as myself."

Palmer told Isaac Bissel where to find Deane. Bissel got back on his horse. Palmer sat at the long table that served as his dining table and desk. He cleared aside a plate and a cold cup of coffee and gathered paper, quill pen, and ink. He took a deep breath and composed the most important letter of his life:

"To all the friends of American Liberty, be it known that this morning before break of day . . ."

There was a knock at the door. It was a man just returning from Lexington. He told Palmer what he knew about the battle. A short time later, Palmer was interrupted again by another man returning from Lexington. He welcomed the intrusions. The more details he included in his letter the better.

Joseph Palmer finished the letter. Palmer and Silas Deane signed the letter. When the ink dried, Palmer handed Isaac Bissel the note.

"Take it to Connecticut," said Palmer.

"I'll take it as far as New York, if I can," replied Bissel.

"You're a good man. Ride fast, Isaac. This is the most important message you'll ever carry."

From Framingham to Springfield, Massachusetts, to Fairfield, Connecticut, Bissel passed on Palmer's letter and people responded with food and a pat on the back to continue. Newspaper editors issued orders to ride to Lexington and gather more information. Angry armed men left their homes and started for Lexington, hoping to meet the British.

The letter Isaac Bissel was carrying was no ordinary letter. It was an alarm that war had begun. It was Palmer's alarm.

Five days later Isaac arrived in New York. When John Holt's *New York Journal* heard the news, it printed a notice that day: SHOTS HAVE BEEN FIRED. MEN KILLED!

Isaac's job was done. A new messenger saddled up and carried Palmer's alarm on to the southern colonies.

JUNE 16, 1775: Washington to Lead Rebel Army. George Washington accepted Congress's nomination to become commander in chief of new colonial army. A quiet, reserved man, he inspired confidence in soldiers on the frontier during French and Indian War. He is considered an expert on warfare and highly respected by fellow congressmen. Named as major generals to assist him were Charles Lee, Israel Putnam, Philip Schuyler, and Artemas Ward. Congress also voted to raise troops in Pennsylvania, Maryland, and Virginia to send to the aid of the army in Massachusetts.

What Joseph Palmer Wrote

To all the friends of American Liberty, be known that this morning before break of day, a brigade consisting of about one thousand or 1200 men landed at Phipp's farm in Cambridge and marched to Lexington where they found a Company of Our Colony Militia in arms upon whom they fired without the least provocation and killed six and wounded four others. By an express this moment from Boston, we find another brigade are now on their march from Boston supposed to be one thousand. The bearer Mr. Isaac Bissel is charged to alarm the country quite to Connecticut and all persons are desired to furnish him with fresh horses, as they may be needed. I have spoke with several persons who have seen the dead and wounded. Pray let the delegates from this colony to Connecticut see this.

They know.

J. Palmer, one of the Committee of Safety

Colonial Newspapers

In 1775, people got their news by talking to their neighbors or reading the paper. There were thirty-seven newspapers in colonial America. All but one were printed once a week. The *Pennsylvania Evening Post* was printed three times a week. It would later be America's first daily paper. Colonial newspapers were smaller than ours. Most were only four pages with three columns per page.

Front-page headlines were rare. Only the most daring editor would be so bold. The front page of a newspaper was for an address to the king, a speech, or the minutes of the assembly. To find the news about the Battles of Lexington and Concord you had to look on page two of most colonial newspapers.

The News Arrives

Here are some dates when news of the Battles of Lexington and Concord were first received:

April 21: *New Hampshire Gazette*, "BLOODY NEWS."

April 26: News reached Baltimore, Maryland. "TO ALL FRIENDS OF AMERICAN LIBERTY."

May 4: News reached Wilmington, North Carolina. The message was sent on with this appeal: "If you should be at a loss for a man and horse the bearer will proceed as far as the Boundary house. For God's sake send the man on without the least delay."

May 31: Almost six weeks after the events at Lexington and Concord, the news finally came to Savannah, Georgia, the most southern city of the colonies.

The Battle of Breed's Hill

"Dig, and dig hard."

Front Row Seats

From the rooftops and second-story windows of Boston homes, people had a clear view of the fighting at Breed's Hill. Ann Hulton, who had been confined in Boston for her safety, said, "From the heights of this place we have a view of the whole town, the harbor and country round for a great extent, and last Saturday I was a spectator of a most awful scene my eyes ever beheld.

"We were exulted in seeing the flight of our enemies [the American militia], but in an hour or two we had occasion to mourn and lament. Dear was the purchase of our safety! In the evening the streets were filled with the wounded and the dying; the sight of which, with the wailing of the women and children over their husbands and fathers, pierced one to the soul."

"Dig, and dig hard," Colonel Prescott commanded his men as they built an earth fort atop Breed's Hill. Prescott's voice was sure, but inside he was nervous.

A spy had brought news that General Gage, the leader of the British forces in Boston, had ordered 7,500 British troops to remove the rebel forces at Breed's Hill. Another battle was brewing.

Almost two months had passed since the Battles of Lexington and Concord on April 19, 1775. It was at Lexington that British forces had shot militiamen in the back as they were withdrawing. The militia had taken their revenge by killing British troops in Concord.

Revenge was not enough. For weeks, rebels traveled from the Massachusetts countryside to set up camp in Cambridge, a town across the Charles River from Boston. The men came with their muskets to show General Gage that they were ready to fight for independence.

Ten thousand men were now gathered near Cambridge. The five thousand British troops stationed there were stuck, outnumbered. General Gage was irritated by this fact. When he learned rebels were building a fort on Breed's Hill, he became furious! If the fort was completed, rebels would control Boston Harbor. They could block British ships from resupplying British troops. They would also be able to protect rebel reinforcements advancing from the

south. Boston would be in danger of being controlled by rebel forces.

But there was a mistake in the rebel plans. Colonel Prescott had chosen Breed's Hill to make his stand against the British. From the hill, Prescott knew his cannons could hit British warships in Boston Harbor. He did not consider that this hill was a poor location to station his soldiers. Breed's Hill was an easy target for British troops. They could attack it from two sides.

The rebel soldiers reshaped the earth into a fort of trenches and walls: 160 feet long by 80 feet wide with walls 6 feet high and a foot thick. They worked to protect themselves from the British troops, the finest trained soldiers in the world.

On the afternoon of June 17, Colonel Prescott's men still had picks and shovels, not rifles, in their hands. A blast shook the earth as British warships sent cannonballs hurling at Breed's Hill. Some of the rebels ran away. The British soldiers were rowed across the river to meet their enemy.

Music Played, Bullets Flew

Colonel Prescott sent two hundred of his colonial troops down to the water's edge. They quickly built a wall of dirt and stones to protect themselves. Eight hundred more men arrived from Cambridge to join them.

When the British soldiers landed at Breed's Hill, their leader, Sir William Howe, surveyed the strength of the militia's defenses and told his troops to sit down to lunch while reinforcements were brought in. The reinforcements arrived under the command of Major Pitcairn, the British officer who had commanded the British troops at Lexington and Concord.

In three divisions totaling about ten thousand men, the British soldiers slowly marched in unison, with their backs straight, carrying 120-pound knapsacks, their bayonets gleaming, their flags flying.

Drum beats and fife music filled the air. The American side beat their drums to the playing of rebel fifes.

The sound of musket fire shattered the pleasing melody. Several British soldiers fell. The shots did not come from Colonel Prescott's men, but from rebels positioned on rooftops in nearby Charlestown. Howe ordered the town burned to the ground. The clear sky was soon clouded with plumes of black smoke.

The British troops moved closer. The American militia watched. Both sides knew their rifles were too inaccurate to kill anyone until they were at close range. The militiamen were commanded to be patient, to refrain from firing till they saw the whites of the enemy's eyes. That was close range.

Colonel Prescott looked out on his British enemy. "Lieutenant Colonel Robinson and Major Woods," he ordered, "take your men and flank the enemy." Later Colonel Prescott wrote, "The enemy advanced and fired very hotly on the fort, and meeting a warm reception, there was a very smart firing on both sides. After a considerable time, finding our ammunition was almost spent I commanded a stop till the enemy advanced within 30 yards, when we gave them such a hot fire they were obliged to retire 150 yards before they could rally and come up again to the attack."

Bayonets in the Bunkers

"Robert Steele, Benjamin Ballard!" came the yell of a rebel sergeant. "Major Moore is badly wounded. You are young and spry, run to the stores and bring some rum. Go as quickly as possible!"

The two rebel boys threw down their guns and went over the hill and down into a nearby store. The store was empty. They called out and a man answered from the cellar. He told the boys, "Keep out of the way of the shot," and then added, "If you want anything in the store, take what you please."

Robert Steele seized a brown two-quart pitcher and filled it from the cask, only to find he had wine. He dumped the wine and from another cask got rum. Benjamin Ballard took a pail of water. Their return was greeted with calls for rum and water, and talk of retreating.

The British, repelled a second time, were advancing for a third time, stepping over a ground blanketed in blood and the bodies of redcoats. Down fell Major Pitcairn, as he led his troops through enemy fire. Major Pitcairn's son, seeing his father fall dead before him, wailed, "I have lost my father." The troops around him called out in chorus, "We have lost our father."

The British troops entered the trenches, bayonets first. The rebel ammunition was nearly exhausted. Few of the militia had bayonets. Men fought with their hands. They fought for their lives. The militia had no choice but to give up Breed's Hill.

The British had won. They had killed 138 of the militia and wounded 276. However, 226 British troops were also killed, 828 were wounded. Said British General Henry Clinton, "It was a dear victory, another such would have ruined us."

The Bigger Hill Gets the Credit

Even though the fighting took place at Breed's Hill, colonists called it "The Battle of Bunker Hill." Today this is still the name that appears in history books. One possible reason: they are adjoining hills and Bunker Hill is bigger.

The British troops entered the trenches, bayonets first.

Daniel Boone Moves West

The horses carried their kettles, dishes, lanterns, and blankets.

Daniel Boone

Daniel Boone had one thing to do before he left the cave on Little Hickman Creek. He drew his knife from the sheath at his side. Digging into the hard surface of the cavern, he gouged his initials and the date: D.B.—1773. This was how he charted distant places he explored. He wiped the blade and joined the men packing their horses. They headed for home.

Boone hated going back to North Carolina. If it weren't for his wife, Rebecca, and their seven children, he would keep on, traveling deeper into the unknown territory west of the Appalachian Mountains. He loved this land. Its mountains were green and beautiful, and its rivers splashed with fish. Buffalo, bear, and deer roamed the forests. A trapper could live well on the sale of beaver and otter pelts. Out here, Boone figured, he could trap all the skins he needed to pay the taxes he owed.

On the trail home, Boone met several men he knew. They had also been exploring the wild land the Indians called Kentucky. They told him of other men who were coming here to settle. The news troubled Boone. It made him restless. He still knew this country better than anyone, but if he waited much longer, he was certain the best land would be taken.

When Boone reached his cabin on the Yadkin River, his mind was made up. He wasted no time finding families who were ready to move west with him. His wife agreed that she and the children would come. She had little choice. Rebecca knew Daniel could not stay put long. She was glad, at least, that some of her own relatives would go with them.

In September, five families were ready to leave. Boone knew that some of them might just try the new country for a while, but he would never turn back. He sold his cabin and everything he could not take with him. On September 25, 1773, his family was packed.

Rebecca Boone was expecting her eighth child. She carried her family's extra clothing in a small drawstring bag. They took their horses, cattle, and only the barest household necessities for a new life. A pack train of horses carried their kettles, butter churns, dishes, lanterns, and blankets.

The trail through the wilderness was narrow and difficult. The pioneers walked single file, leading the animals. Only the littlest children and women were allowed to ride. Ahead, they would cross the Blue Ridge, Appalachian, and Cumberland mountains.

The pioneers walked single file, leading the animals.

The adventurers went north into Virginia and then west again, following an Indian trail called Warrior's Path. For almost two weeks, they met no real danger. But they were running short of flour. Boone decided to send his son James and Henry Russell, both sixteen, to a settlement not far away, where he hoped they could get more food. A man named Drake, a hired hand, two young boys, and two black slaves went with them to help. The families planned to meet the boys again farther along the trail.

On October 9, one hundred fifty miles from home, the main group reached Cumberland Gap, a natural pass through the mountains. The next morning they expected to be in Kentucky. The weary families pitched their camps, built fires, ate supper, and spread their blankets on the ground.

James Boone and Henry Russell made their camp that night beside Walden's Creek, where their animals could get water. They did not know their families were only three miles ahead. With wolves howling in the mountains, the boys finally fell asleep.

Shawnees in war paint crept silently through the brush as the night sky lightened to early morning gray. No one awoke in time. The Indians attacked the sleeping boys with bows and arrows and tomahawks. Drake and the two little ones died quickly. One of the black men, struck in the forehead by a tomahawk, leapt across the stream and hid. He was found days later, wandering in confusion.

James Boone and Henry Russell suffered the most. Paralyzed by arrows, they lay helpless as the Indians tortured them and left them to die.

The horrible massacre was discovered later that morning, when one of the men from Boone's camp decided to turn back. He reached Walden's Creek at daybreak, aghast at the bloody scene before him. He rode quickly back to break the news to the others. In shock and fear, the families returned to bury their five dead loved ones. This wild land was too much for them. They stood quietly beside the graves they had covered with rocks to keep wolves away. They decided to turn back.

Only Daniel Boone would not. He had nothing to return to. He had sold everything to make this expedition. But winter was coming, and he could not take his family into the wilderness alone. One of the families offered him an empty cabin in Virginia. The Boones went there. Alone in the wilderness, they spent the long cold months in sorrow, thinking of their beloved James.

When spring finally came, Boone returned to James's grave. Wolves had pawed at it, so Daniel dug it deeper. Then he set out once again, to warn other pioneers of angry Indians who might attack suddenly. Despite the danger, Boone would never stop exploring. Someday soon, he vowed, he would take his family back to the land the Indians called Kentucky.

No Trespassing

Long before Daniel Boone began scouting west of the Appalachian Mountains, the British proclaimed it forbidden territory. At the end of the war against the French, the British Proclamation of 1763 gave a vast piece of land west of the colonies to the Indians. To keep other people off the land, the proclamation ruled that white men could not buy it from the Indians, hunt on it, or even explore it for settlement.

The proclamation did not stop Boone, however. He was a friend to many Shawnees and Cherokees. He hunted with them, and they trusted him. Black Fish, a Shawnee chief, adopted him as a son. The name Boone was given did not describe his muscular build, dark wavy hair, blue eyes, or slightly Roman nose. Old records say that Black Fish named him "Wide Mouth."

The Indians respected Boone, but they would not let most white men use their land. When the royal governors of Virginia and North Carolina heard rumors that families like the Boones were moving there anyway, they called it lawlessness. But with rebellion breaking out in the northern colonies, the British could hardly worry much about the Kentucky wilderness.

The Shawnee crept silently.

Build a Fort

Look at this drawing of Fort Boonesborough. What materials could you use to build a model of the fort? See what you can come up with to make a sturdy, natural fortress. Can you improve on the design?

What You Need:

Something for the foundation—a large cookie sheet or piece of plywood; red potter's clay for a base to support the fort's walls; brown grocery bags; white glue; Popsicle sticks or twigs to make the walls, masking tape or duct tape to make gate hinges.

1. Build a 2-inch-thick clay base on the platform. Make the four outer walls of the fort by pushing sticks into the clay base about 1 inch deep. Leave openings in two walls for the fort entrances. Make the cabins inside the fort with rows of shorter sticks pushed into the soft clay.

2. Glue sticks together to make the fort gates. Attach them to the main walls by making hinges of strong tape that will allow the gates to open and close.

3. Build four small lookout towers with rows of sticks glued onto brown paper foundations. Support the lookout towers with posts made from taller sticks. Make a roof to cover each tower.

4. Find moss and twigs to make grass and trees inside the fort. Does it need anything else? Can you add a river or hills around the outside of the fort? Do you have miniature action figures or animals that can live in it?

The Beginning of Fort Boonesborough

After a feast of bear meat, roasted corn, and rum, Daniel Boone, thirty men, and two black slave women set off for Kentucky in March 1775. They crossed rivers, climbed mountains, and chopped through forests, clearing the road. Sometimes they widened Indian trails and buffalo paths. They often rode into country that white men had never seen before.

It took them three weeks to chop through 250 miles of wilderness. On April 1, 1775, they reached their destination. Stopping where the Kentucky River and Otter Creek joined, the men named the future settlement Boonesborough, to honor their leader.

Each man received enough silver shillings to buy 420 acres of land. They held a drawing to select lots. Then they started building a fortress for protection against Indian attacks. Fort Boonesborough began to take shape. At each corner stood a lookout tower. Two heavy log gates could close against danger. Five small cabins were built inside the stockade along one wall. When they finished, log walls twelve feet high would keep everyone safe.

After the little cabins were built, the men cleared a spot to plant cucumber and corn seeds before it got too warm. Then they started building thirty larger cabins in a strip between the fort and the forest. Soon more men began arriving at Boonesborough. Daniel Boone preferred hunting to carpentry. He brought the settlers fresh meat.

When the summer days grew shorter and the weather began to cool, Boone rode back to South Carolina to get Rebecca and their seven children. At last, they were moving to Kentucky.

The new fort must have looked crude to Rebecca. The first wall, with the five little cabins, was still only half finished. A pack of dogs barked noisily, and autumn fires clouded the air with smoke. She and her daughters, Jemima and baby Sarah, and two black women were the only females so far. But Fort Boonesborough was their new home, and Rebecca wasted no time making her family's cabin comfortable.

They planted cucumbers and corn.

Benjamin Franklin: Runaway Genius

Ben Franklin at the press.

Did you know that one of the most famous men in American history, and one of the smartest, went to school for only two years? When he was eight, his parents put him in school. But there were seventeen children in Ben's family, and classes were expensive. He had to quit school when he was ten. But Ben continued to read endlessly. Books gave him ideas about nearly everything, from science to philosophy.

Growing up in Boston, where he was born in 1706, Benjamin Franklin longed to go to sea, but his father had other ideas. He was a candle-maker and a soapmaker. He taught Ben to pour the hot wax into the candle molds and to make the wicks. Ben was bored. Mr. Franklin worried that Ben might run away to sea if he did not find something more interesting to do.

After work, Ben and his father often went for walks around their neighborhood. They passed men loading ships, felling trees, and building new homes. Mr. Franklin watched his son's face for a sign of curiosity or interest. Nothing Ben saw looked appealing.

Finally, his father decided that since Ben loved books so much, he should learn the printing business. Ben's older half-brother could teach him. America had only two newspapers then, and James Franklin published one of them.

When he was only twelve, Benjamin Franklin reluctantly signed a contract that bound him to his brother for nine years. At least as a "printer's devil," he would learn a useful trade. Ben liked setting type. At night he could borrow and read many good books. But he and his older brother argued all the time. After a few years, Ben was sick of James's bossiness. He knew his father would not let him quit. So he decided to run away. He made up a story about needing to leave Boston secretly.

Ben sold some of his books to buy passage on a sloop sailing to New York. When he arrived, a printer told him there might be a job in Philadelphia. Ben started off again. In Philadelphia, he found a job helping a printer. When he returned to Boston a few weeks later, he wore new clothes and carried a pocketwatch. Five sterling silver pieces jingled in his pocket. The most valuable item he brought was a letter from the governor of Philadelphia. The governor wanted Ben to come back and help start a new printing shop.

At first, Ben's father said "no" to this plan. But a few weeks later he changed his mind. He realized what a good opportunity this might be for his son. He and James tore up the contract that bound young Benjamin. At eighteen, Benjamin Franklin set off for the city that would be his new home.

DECEMBER 23, 1775: British Order Colonial Ports Closed. King George ruled today that the colonies are closed to all international trade, effective March 1776. The king reportedly took this step in reaction to colonial boycotts of imported British goods.

The Inventor

Perhaps Franklin sat reading by the fire one cold, rainy night when he got another bright idea. In those days, fireplaces were big and smoky. They gobbled up piles of wood but gave off little heat. Franklin studied the way hot and cold air circulated around the fireplace. Then he designed the "Philadelphia stove" (later called the Franklin stove). Made of cast iron and shaped like a box, it fit inside the fireplace, with the grate extending out into the room. The Franklin stove had vents on the sides. The vents allowed warm air to flow out and heat the room faster, more evenly, and with less smoke than a fireplace.

Franklin's Philadelphia Stove.

Another of Franklin's ideas improved mail delivery. In Franklin's time, mail was delivered in the colonies by stagecoach. Postage was paid at the post office by the person who received the letter. Postage fees were based on how far the letter traveled. Postal clerks often disagreed with customers about delivery distance and how much they should pay.

MARCH 18, 1776: Washington Captures Redcoats. More British soldiers arrived in Boston today, and were immediately captured by Washington. British did not know the army they came to rescue sailed away yesterday. Washington surrounded the city on March 17. British driven out without a single weapon fired.

When Franklin was appointed postmaster of all the colonies, he invented a machine—an odometer—to measure the mileage between towns. Franklin rode from town to town with the machine attached to the hub of his carriage wheel. He hauled a cart of stones and dropped one stone along the highway at each mile of distance he covered. Franklin's highway milestones soon put an end to arguments over mail rates.

He dropped a stone every mile.

When people think of Franklin the inventor, they probably remember him as the man who "invented electricity." His curiosity about electricity began in 1748. That year, he sold his printing business so he could retire and work on scientific inventions. He was forty-two years old. He went to Boston and attended a lecture given by Dr. Archibald Spencer.

Dr. Spencer showed the audience some glass tubes with electricity stored in them. Franklin was amazed. He bought several tubes and other equipment, and built a laboratory in his house on Market Street in Philadelphia. Whenever he learned something new about electricity, he wrote a report on it. No one yet knew what to do with electrical power, but scientists everywhere were fascinated by it.

Franklin believed that lightning was electricity stored in the clouds. He wanted to capture it, but he needed something tall enough to get near the clouds. Even the church steeples in the city were too low. Franklin had another idea. In 1752, he asked his son William to help him test it.

During a thunderstorm they went to an open field to launch a kite. The kite had a pointed

The Leather Apron Club

Before the Revolution began, Benjamin Franklin amazed people around the world with his ideas and experiments. His genius led to endless inventions, large and small. In 1727 he and some of his friends started a group that met on Friday nights. Most of the men, like Franklin, were skilled craftsmen. When a craftsman worked, he wore a leather apron that held tools and protected his clothes. Franklin and his friends called their group the Leather Apron Club. They met to talk about philosophical ideas that interested them. The club grew into what is now called the American Philosophical Association.

Franklin's club ordered 375 books from London. Many of these books were written by John Locke, an Englishman famous for his new political ideas. As one member finished a book, he passed it along to another. This new idea of lending books caught on everywhere. Soon other "lending libraries" were formed.

metal wire fastened to its tip. The metal would attract electricity and conduct, or carry, it down the wet kite string. Tied to the end of the string was a metal key.

Because electricity was such a new science, Benjamin Franklin did not know exactly how dangerous it could be. A very strong bolt of lightning might have killed him and his son. Fortunately, he *did* know it would be dangerous to handle the wet kite string. He held the kite by another string tied to the key. During the storm, he and his son stood safely inside a shed so the string they were holding would not get wet during the storm.

When lightning flashed, it traveled down the kite string and into the key. When Franklin and his son placed their hands *near* the key, sparks flew from the string. The sparks proved that lightning and electricity were identical.

For his discoveries about electricity, Franklin was honored everywhere. He received awards and special degrees from colleges and scientific academies in America, England, and France. In Germany and Russia they called him "the man who took fire from the heavens."

Benjamin's Acrostic

An acrostic is a poem or several lines of verse containing a pattern of letters—usually the first letter in each line—that spell one or more words.

Ben Franklin's uncle (also named Benjamin Franklin) wrote an acrostic about how Ben should behave. Each verse in the acrostic began with one of the letters in his nephew's name.

Notice that he used an "i" instead of the "j" in Benjamin. Can you guess why? Was he a poor speller? Maybe he couldn't think of a good word that began with "j."

Look at the example below. Now try writing an acrostic using your name.

B-e to thy parents an obedient son,
E-ach day let duty constantly be done.
N-ever give way to sloth or lust or pride,
I-f free you'd be from thousand ills beside;
A-bove all ills, be sure avoid the shelf;
M-an's danger lies in Satan, sin, and self.
I-n virtue, learning, wisdom progress make,
N-e'er shrink at suffering for thy Saviour's sake.
F-raud and all falsehood in thy dealings flee,
R-eligious always in thy station be,
A-dore the maker of thy inward part.
N-ow's the accepted time; give God thy heart.
K-eep a good conscience, 'tis a constant friend;
L-ike judge and witness this thy act attend.
I-n heart, with bended knee, alone, adore
N-one but the Three-in-One forevermore.

Franklin and his son flew their kite in a lightning storm.

The Story of Phillis Wheatley

The little girl had never known anything so dreadful.

The little African girl screamed as she was grabbed by a gruff man who was shouting in a strange language. Kicking and twisting, she tried to break free. Suddenly, her cheek felt on fire from the sting of the man's hand across it. She felt something tight and scratchy around her ankles. Then the world went blank.

When the little girl could open her eyes again, she was horrified. She was trapped in darkness, deep in the hold of a creaky wooden ship named the *Phillis*. The ship's floor swayed up and down, pushing her into a crowd of people—African men, women, and children—all chained together. No one could move.

The air was hot and stinking. The smell made the little girl's stomach turn inside out. People were moaning with sickness. Other men, like the one who had grabbed her away from her family, came down into the dim hold, carrying whips and shouting angrily. The little girl was frightened. She had never known anything so dreadful.

After several terrible weeks at sea, the *Phillis* reached the wharf at Boston. The men with whips yelled and shoved the Africans into a line on the dock. The little girl looked tiny and frail beside the women, still wearing their heavy leg chains.

Standing at the long pier, the tailor John Wheatley and his wife, Susanna, spotted the little girl. The captain told them he had named her Phillis, for the slave ship that carried her thousands of miles from her home in Africa to the colonies. Susanna worried that the child was sick. She and her husband bought Phillis "for a trifle." They probably paid about ten pounds sterling for her. They gave her their last name, as people who bought slaves often did, and took her home.

Phillis was a child of seven or eight years old in 1761 when the slave traders brought her to America. We think Phillis was born on the Gambia River, in Gambia, on the western coast of Africa.

In Boston, the Wheatleys took good care of her. Mary Wheatley, their sixteen-year-old daughter, taught her the alphabet and the sounds of the letters. Phillis learned to read Bible passages and English poetry. As she grew up, she began to express her own thoughts about God, freedom, and slavery in poetry. Some of her poems criticized the British for their taxes on the colonies.

The Wheatleys realized Phillis was exceptionally smart. In 1773, she traveled to London with Nathaniel Wheatley, her owner's son. They took more than seventy of Phillis's poems with them. In London, her poetry was published in a little book called *Poems on Various Subjects, Religious and Moral.* Phillis Wheatley became the first black poet in America.

The Wheatleys loved Phillis like a daughter. It seemed wrong to keep her as a slave. When she returned from London a few months later, they gave her the freedom that had been taken from her.

A Hymn to the Evening
by Phillis Wheatley

Soon as the sun forsook the eastern main
The pealing thunder shook the heav'nly plain;
Majestic grandeur! From the zephyr's wing,
Exhales the incense of the blooming Spring.
Soft purl the streams, the birds renew their
    notes,
And through the air their mingled music floats.

Through all the heav'ns what beauteous dies are
    spread!
But the west glories in the deepest red:
So may our breaths with ev'ry virtue glow,
The living temples of our God below!

Fill'd with the praise of him who gives the light,
And draws the sable curtains of the night,
Let placid slumbers sooth each weary mind,
At morn to wake more heav'nly, more refin'd,
So shall the labours of the day begin
More pure, more guarded from the snares of
    sin.
Night's leaden sceptre seals my drowsy eyes,
Then cease, my song, til fair *Aurora* rise.

Sir [George Washington]

I have taken the freedom to address your Excellency in the enclosed poem, and entreat your acceptance, though I am not insensible of its inaccuracies. Your being appointed by the Grand Continental Congress to be Generalissimo of the armies of North America, together with the fame of your virtues, excite sensations not easy to suppress. Your generosity, therefore, I presume, will pardon the attempt. Wishing your Excellency all possible success in the great cause you are so generously engaged in. I am,
    Your Excellency's most obedient humble servant,
    Phillis Wheatley
October 26, 1775
(Phillis Wheatley may have sent her letter to General Washington. This version appeared in the *Virginia Gazette* on March 20, 1776.)

JANUARY 9, 1776: *Common Sense* **Spreads Talk of Revolution. A radical pamphlet that calls King George a "Royal Brute" was published in Philadelphia and is being widely circulated among the colonies. Criticizing the unlimited power of kings, copies sold out quickly. Colonists troubled and deeply inspired by anonymous essay that demands the right for people to govern themselves.**

Phillis Wheatley

FREEDOM, BUT NOT FOR ALL

Many people in the colonies believed freedom was a God-given right that everyone should enjoy. But in the eighteenth century, they did not really mean *all* people.

African slaves, shipped to the colonies and sold to white masters, were the largest group whose freedom was taken away by others. In 1776, nearly two and a half million slaves in America were considered less than human and were treated as property.

Other people, too, knew how it felt to live without freedom. Hundreds of white people sailed to the colonies from Europe without a penny in their pockets. If they couldn't pay their ship passage, they, too, became like slaves. They were usually treated better than blacks, but they had to work for someone else for five to ten years, to repay their travel debts. They were "bound" to work, and were called "indentured servants."

Tom Paine's Little Book

Tom Paine's little book caused a huge commotion. People read it and passed it to their friends. Everywhere they argued about his fiery ideas.

Why did *Common Sense* cause such excitement? Tom Paine chose just the right words to express the ideas everyone was already thinking.

People were startled by these brave words. But their response was "Yes, yes!" "He's right, that's how it is!" The American Revolution began like a brush fire, smoldering away, growing hotter and smokier. Paine's words acted like a breeze, fanning the fire until it exploded into uncontrolled flames.

What did Paine say to light the fire of revolution? Paine began with ideas most people already agreed with: "Society is a blessing, but government, even in its best state, is . . . a necessary evil."

Long ago, Paine said, there were no kings and no wars. Kings threw things into confusion. A man became a king only by being *born* to it. Paine said this ancient custom caused most of the trouble in the world. He argued that the colonies did not need such a ruler.

He gave reasons: "The nearer any government approaches to [independence], the less business there is for a king." He criticized what kings do: "In England a king hath little more to do than to make war and give away places. . . . A pretty business indeed for a man to be [paid] eight hundred thousand sterling a year . . . and [be] worshipped [in] the bargain!"

Paine complained that the distance between the mother country and the colonies added more problems: "To be always running . . . four thousand miles with a [story or a question], waiting . . . five months for an answer, which, when [received], [needs] . . . six more to explain it, will [soon seem ridiculous]. There was a time when it was proper, and there is a proper time for it to cease."

He said England was too small to rule over a huge country like America. "There is something absurd in supposing a continent [can be] governed by an island."

Finally, he said it was too late to turn back. He dared people to believe in their absolute right to freedom and independence.

"The sun never shined on a cause of greater worth," Thomas Paine wrote. Some of his final words were: "The last cord now is broken. . . . Everything that is right or reasonable pleads for separation. . . .

"The weeping voice of nature cries, *'TIS TIME TO PART'*."

The thought of independence was frightening, shocking, and terribly risky. What if it didn't work? What would the king do to people who opposed him? Such serious questions had no simple answers.

As *Common Sense* spread through the colonies, more and more copies were needed. Paine gave the printing rights to the new colonial government in Philadelphia. He could have become rich selling it himself. By letting the government print and sell almost half a million copies of the booklet for two shillings each, he donated nearly one million dollars to America's struggle for freedom.

Thomas Paine

Thomas Paine was a man who dared to write what other people were afraid to say. In England he wrote a pamphlet criticizing the low pay of customs agents. In 1774 he came to Philadelphia as a writer for *Pennsylvania Magazine*. His articles on improving education and care for the elderly were so popular that readership tripled in three months. Late in 1775 he wrote a history of the conflict between the colonies and England. It was a forty-seven-page booklet he called *Common Sense*. In 1776, thousands of copies were printed and read by every colonist who cared about freedom.

Brother Benjamin: A Game

American children played a game in the eighteenth century called Brother Jonathan. The object was to toss tuppenny pieces onto a board, aiming for the high point areas. This version, Brother Benjamin, calls for a board in the shape of the colonies, and American copper pennies. The game is for one or more players.

What You Need:

Five pennies per player. A piece of poster board or cardboard, pencil, and permanent marker (optional). Using the map of the colonies on page 14 in this book as your guide, draw the thirteen colonies on the poster board. Print the names of the colonies and give each one a point value as follows: New Hampshire, 10; Massachusetts, 10; Connecticut, 10; Rhode Island, 20; New York, 3; Pennsylvania, 3; New Jersey, 15; Delaware, 20; Maryland, 10; Virginia, 5; North Carolina, 3; South Carolina, 5; Georgia, 5. (After you draw and label it, go over the map with a permanent marker.)

How to Play:

Place the board on the floor. Before you start, decide a total that will win the game. Standing at a set distance from the board, each player tosses a penny on the board. Highest point decides starting order.

The first player tosses his or her five pennies on the board, and adds up the total points. A penny that lands on a line does not count but is not retossed. Players take turns tossing their pennies until one person reaches the game total. Remaining players finish the last round, and the player with the highest total is declared winner.

Words to Change the World

They were the most important words he would ever write.

Thomas Jefferson was a long way from home. He sat at a small portable desk in a room on the second floor of a house at the corner of Market and Seventh streets in Philadelphia. His tall, slender body was hunched over the desk as he wrote, crossed out, and wrote again.

Jefferson frowned as he thought about the words. They were the most important words he would ever write in his life. They were words that would change the world and the lives of people everywhere. When he finished, Jefferson had written only 1,800 words, but it had taken him seventeen long days to write them.

Jefferson had left his mansion in Virginia to attend the Second Continental Congress in Philadelphia. The members of the congress had voted to break away from Great Britain and the king, and become independent states. Now they needed to explain this shattering decision to their countrymen and to the rest of the world. They believed that the best man to convey their beliefs about freedom was Thomas Jefferson. The document Jefferson wrote is called the Declaration of Independence. This is how it begins:

"When, in the course of human events, it becomes necessary for one people to dissolve the political bands which have connected them with another, and to assume among the powers of the earth, the separate and equal station to which the laws of nature and of nature's God entitle them, a decent respect to the opinions of mankind requires that they should declare the causes which impel them to the separation.

"We hold these truths to be self-evident: that all men are created equal; that they are endowed by their creator with certain unalienable rights; that among these are life,

This is the first known American political cartoon. It was drawn and printed by Benjamin Franklin in 1754 for his newspaper the Pennsylvania Gazette, *and it shows the colonies as segments of a serpent. The segment marked N.E. stands for the colonies in New England (Connecticut, Rhode Island, Massachusetts, and New Hampshire). Which colonies are missing from the cartoon?*

liberty, and the pursuit of happiness; that to secure these rights, governments are instituted among men, deriving their just powers from the consent of the governed; that whenever any form of government becomes destructive of these ends, it is the right of the people to alter or to abolish it, and to institute new government, laying its foundation on such principles, and organizing its powers in such form, as to them shall seem most likely to effect their safety and happiness."

WHO WAS THIS MAN JEFFERSON?

Thomas Jefferson was tall, slender, and handsome, with thick, chestnut-colored hair. He was devoted to his family and did not like being away from home too long. Yet he felt it was his duty to attend the Second Continental Congress. When it met, Jefferson was thirty-three years old, the second youngest member there.

Jefferson was born in Virginia in 1743. When he was fourteen, his father died. His father left money specifically for Thomas's education. He attended William and Mary College in Virginia and then studied law. He was a member of the Virginia parliament, and later became the governor of Virginia.

Jefferson did not like debating. But he was genius at expressing his thoughts in writing. His arguments were clear and convincing. His brilliance brought him world fame.

Jefferson was also a master at figuring out ways to improve life. He developed a new plow and better farming methods at his estate near Charlottesville, Virginia. His thirty-five-room home, "Monticello," held many of his inventions. He designed folding chairs and swivel chairs.

Jefferson also invented a pendulum calendar clock that never needed winding. He built a special elevator into the wall of his dining room, so servants in the downstairs kitchen could send hot food to the table without using the stairs.

His improvements usually saved time for other things. For example, Jefferson couldn't write during the long ride between Philadelphia and Monticello. But he arrived in Philadelphia in 1776 with an idea for a most useful invention—a portable lap desk—that he could travel with.

He designed the writing desk with a drawer for paper. Small compartments held inkwells, quills, penholders, and penpoints. The drawer had a decorative brass handle and locked with a key. The top of the desk was a writing surface that could also hold a book at six different angles. It folded flat when it wasn't being used.

Jefferson took his portable desk design to Benjamin Randolph, a Philadelphia cabinet-maker. Randolph built the desk from mahogany, a rich, dark wood with a pleasing grain. The result was a fine piece of furniture that Jefferson treasured for the rest of his life.

Where Is It Now?

When Jefferson died in 1826, his lap desk was given to his grandson-in-law, Joseph Coolidge, Jr., who lived in Boston. Joseph kept the desk for fifty-five years. In 1880, Congress accepted it as a gift. You can see it when you visit the National Museum of American History at the Smithsonian Institution.

Thomas Jefferson's famous lap desk

JUNE 7, 1776: Lee Calls for Independence. Richard Henry Lee, Congressman from Virginia, asked fellow delegates to adopt a motion "That these United Colonies are, and of right ought to be, free and independent States." Lee's proposal followed calls for independence from North Carolina (April 12) and Virginia (May 15).

The Colonies Vote for Freedom

Richard Henry Lee spoke in a clear voice.

On June 7, 1776, Richard Henry Lee, another delegate from Virginia, stood up and spoke in a clear voice. He said, "The united colonies are, and of right ought to be, free and independent States."

For many days, the congress debated Lee's call for independence. On July 2, the members voted. Lee's resolution passed by twelve votes. (The colonists in New York had asked their delegate not to vote.)

During the debates, the congress selected five men to write a formal announcement that the colonies had chosen freedom. Benjamin Franklin, John Adams, Robert E. Livingston, and Roger Sherman were on the committee. The fifth member, Thomas Jefferson, had a reputation for clear thought and fine writing. Adams praised Jefferson and asked him to write this important document.

On July 1, 1776, the delegates in the congress listened to Jefferson's words. The Declaration was discussed, debated, and revised. Jefferson was unhappy with some of the changes, but he did not argue. Finally, John Hancock, the president of the congress, insisted that everyone go along with it. "We must hang together," Hancock urged.

"Yes," replied Benjamin Franklin, "we must indeed all hang together, or most assuredly we shall all hang separately."

On July 2, the delegates voted to accept the Declaration of Independence. It was recopied with the changes and taken to John Dunlap, a

JULY 2, 1776: It's Official! Congress Votes Yes. After nearly a month of debates over Lee's resolution and the Declaration of Independence, the congress formally dissolved ties to Great Britain. New United Colonies established as free and independent States.

Philadelphia printer. He printed twenty-four copies of the document on parchment. Late in the afternoon of July 4, 1776, the original was signed first by John Hancock, president of the Continental Congress, and Charles Thomson, the secretary.

All fifty-six delegates signed their names to the bottom of the page. In signing the Declaration of Independence, the members of the congress promised each other their "Lives . . . Fortunes, and . . . Sacred Honor." They took their new freedom seriously.

Congress had copies of the Declaration printed as handbills. They were delivered to the colonial armies and read to the soldiers. At first, few people knew that Jefferson had written it. Later, when they found out who the writer was, Jefferson's reputation as a genius grew.

Thomas Jefferson looked back on those days in Philadelphia with pride. Writing the Declaration of Independence, he said, was one of the greatest accomplishments of his life. He had not tried to invent new ideas when he wrote it. He simply wanted it to express the feelings in the minds of all Americans.

John Adams was born in 1735 in Quincy, Massachusetts. Throughout his long life he was known for his courage and his intense devotion to American independence. In 1789, he was elected George Washington's vice president, and he became the country's second president when Washington refused a second term. His eldest son, John Quincy Adams, became our sixth president. John Adams and Thomas Jefferson both died on the same day, July 4, 1826, fifty years after the signing of the Declaration of Independence!

The First Fourth of July

Colonel Nixon read the Declaration of Independence to the hushed crowd.

When the Founding Fathers finally had time to celebrate the new nation's birthday, the Fourth of July had come and gone. It was July 8 when Colonel John Nixon stood on the speaker's platform on the lawn of Carpenters' Hall in Philadelphia and read the Declaration of Independence to the hushed crowd that had gathered.

First ever to read the Declaration in public, Nixon was a popular Philadelphia businessman and a military commander. He came home from one battle in time for the celebration and then went back to another.

On that summer day in Philadelphia, his reading ended with round after round of gunpowder fired into the air by the militia. Church bells rang out, but none as loudly as the State Bell atop Carpenters' Hall. Their new names—Liberty Bell and Independence Hall—would forever honor this historic event.

If John Adams had chosen in 1776, July 2 would have become our most important national holiday. Why? That was the date the congress passed Richard Henry Lee's resolution saying the colonies should declare themselves free. Instead, we celebrate July 4, the day the Declaration of Independence was signed.

Adams hoped the Fourth of July would be honored across the land, with "shows, games, sports, guns, bells, bonfires, and illuminations." Traditions have changed since those days, and most cities have safer rules for celebrations. Are any of Adams's suggestions forbidden in your town?

An old-fashioned Fourth of July began with a parade. (In many communities it still does.) Men and women wearing military uniforms marched proudly down the street, carrying the American flag. A military band followed, filling the air with music and drumming. After a salute of firearms and patriotic speeches by decorated heroes, cannonfire boomed like thunder. When the ceremonies ended, everyone played games and enjoyed icy drinks. In the evening, men and women dressed in their finest for an evening of dancing and celebrating the nation's freedom and remembering the sacrifices that won it.

For families today, the Fourth of July might include a parade, a camping trip, or a picnic, and watching fireworks glitter at twilight. Ask your favorite adults how they celebrated our national holiday when they were kids. How do you spend the Fourth of July?

Old Glory Ice Cream

Next Fourth of July, surprise your family with an ice cream treat in honor of the colonial American flag, and noisemakers that won't get you thrown into the Boston jail!

What You Need:

One half-gallon vanilla ice cream, three cups fresh strawberry halves, one-half cup white frosting, blue food coloring, a small package of yogurt-dipped raisins or white candy.

1. Mix several drops of food coloring into the frosting to make it a deep blue color. If the frosting gets too thick as you're working, thin it with a little milk or water.

2. Soften the ice cream and spread it in a 9-inch by 13-inch pan. (Keep it in the freezer until it is good and hard.)

3. In the upper left corner of the ice cream pan, brush the blue frosting into a rectangle as the background for the stars. Make a circle of thirteen white candy "stars" in the center of the blue section.

4. Make strawberry stripes by placing the berries side-by-side, cut side down, in rows along the length of the pan. Begin and end with red stripes. (The size of the strawberries will determine how many red stripes you will have—probably four to six.) Put Old Glory into the freezer until your other projects are done.

THE PRINTER WAS A LADY

By January 1777, the Declaration of Independence had been printed seven times. But on January 18 that year, Congress decided that each state in the new union should have its own official copy of the Declaration of Independence, including the names of the original delegates.

Congress was meeting in Baltimore, because the British had taken Philadelphia. It made sense to find a Baltimore printer. Such a person was Mary Katharine Goddard. She had learned printing from her younger brother William, who had published the *Pennsylvania Chronicle*, the paper started by Benjamin Franklin's Leather Apron Club.

Perhaps Congress chose her to print the Declaration because her work was of excellent quality. She was also well known. In addition to printing her own paper, the *Maryland Journal*, Mary Katharine Goddard was postmistress of Baltimore from 1775 to 1789.

How can you tell one edition of the Declaration of Independence from another? There are several clues. The original Declaration was signed by each delegate, in general geographic order, starting with delegates of the northern colonies on the left side. The "official" Goddard printing lists the delegates' names in neat columns beside the states they represented. The very bottom of the document says "Baltimore, In Maryland: Printed by Mary Katharine Goddard."

Independence Day Noisemakers

Revolutionary Rattles

What You Need:

(For each rattle) one empty bathroom tissue roll, one tablespoon raw popcorn or dry beans, one 10-inch by 12-inch piece of crepe paper or fabric, white glue, two 8-inch lengths of string.

1. Center the tissue roll on the long side of the fabric. Squeeze glue along the top of the roll, and bring the edge of the fabric up. Press the fabric onto the glue. Roll the fabric around the tissue tube and glue it at the other edge. Wipe off any extra glue.

2. Gather the fabric at one end of the tube and tie it with a firm knot and a bow.

3. Fill the other end with popcorn or beans, and tie it closed with a knot and a bow. After the glue has dried, shake the rattle with all your might.

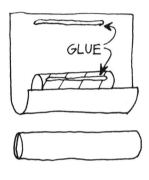  

Patriotic Poppers

What You Need:

One sheet of blank white paper or newspaper for each popper (the larger the paper, the louder the "pop").

1. Fold the paper in half lengthwise. Spread it open again and fold the four corners so the points nearly touch at the middle.

2. Fold the paper in half again on the first fold. It should have a long point at each end and a straight open edge across the top.

3. Bring the end points together and fold the paper in half across the middle.

4. Fold the pointed ends in half, covering the non-pointed ends.

5. Hold the popper by the two points, with the folded-in paper along the bottom. To make it pop, snap your hand forward. The folded paper inside will "pop" out with a loud noise. Tuck that paper inside and snap it again.

When you've rattled and popped until you're out of breath and sweaty, cool off with a dish of Old Glory ice cream.

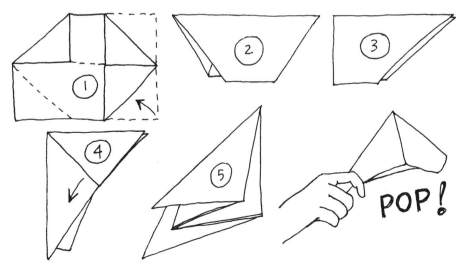

Lost and Found: An Original Copy

In 1989, a man in Pennsylvania went to a flea market. He bought an old painting in a wooden frame. At home, he took the frame off the painting and discovered a copy of the Declaration of Independence behind the picture. After tests, experts told him the document was authentic.

It is one of twenty-four copies that were printed during the night of July 4, 1776. Twenty-one of them belong to museums, and three are owned privately. The Pennsylvania man sold his at an art auction in 1991 for nearly two and a half million dollars!

The Beating of the Distant Drum

Sarah saw the empty houses and shops with boarded windows.

One autumn morning in 1776, Sarah Wister climbed onto the backseat of the wagon beside her sister Elizabeth. Sarah, the oldest of the Wister children, had just turned sixteen in July. This morning Sarah had helped her mother pack the food and clothing they would need. She had said good-bye to Deborah Norris and Sally Jones, her two best friends. Now she settled her three younger sisters and her baby brother on the hard wooden seat and tried to get comfortable for the long ride. She looked back at the tall brick house they were about to leave.

Every summer since she could remember, Sarah's family left Philadelphia to go to the country where it was cooler. They had just returned, but now they were leaving once again. Her father said the British might attack Philadelphia. He had decided to take his family to their aunt's farm, where they would be safer. Sarah knew that her father would not join the militia and fight the British. The Wisters were Quakers. They believed war was wrong. But Daniel Wister said if he could help defend America in peaceful ways, he would.

Other families were leaving Philadelphia, and more would follow. As the wagon rattled over the cobblestone streets of the city, Sarah saw empty houses and shops with boards across their windows. She hoped they could all return soon. She wondered if her aunt's house would be safe from the fighting.

At the farm, Sarah's aunt, Mrs. Foulke, and her children Jesse, Priscilla, and Lydia welcomed their cousins. Sarah's father put the wagon in the barn. Next to the barn was the cookhouse, a small kitchen separate from the living quarters. The big house, with several bedrooms upstairs, had room for everyone. As soon as Sarah unpacked, she and her cousin Lydia went for a walk in the woods. After supper, when the dishes were washed, they went upstairs and tried on each other's dresses.

Sarah Starts a Journal

Every day the girls helped with babysitting, sewing, and housework. When Sarah was alone, she read or embroidered. She wanted to write to her friends Deborah and Sally, but the war made it difficult to send mail. Then she had an idea. In a little notebook, Sarah would keep a journal. When she saw her friends again, she would share what she had written. On September 25, 1777, she began writing to her friend Deborah Norris in her small notebook. She had exciting news to tell:

"Yesterday two Virginia officers called at our house and informed us that the British Army had crossed the Schuylkill River. Presently another person stopped and said that General Washington and [his] Army were near Pottsgrove. Well, thee may be sure we were sufficiently scared. However, the road was very still till evening."

But that night, armed colonists stopped at the farmhouse on their way to fight the British. She described her fear:

"About seven o'clock we heard a great noise and to the door all went. A large number of Waggons with about three hundred of the Philadelphia Militia appeared. They begged for drink and several pushed into the house. One of those that entered was a little tipsy and had a mind to be saucy. I then thought it time for me to retreat. Picture me running in one door and out another, all in a shake with fear. But after a while, seeing the officers appear gentlemanly and the Soldiers civil, I calmed down, though my teeth rattled and my hands shook like an aspen leaf."

The next afternoon a neighbor warned the two families that they would soon see British soldiers. The British, led by General William Howe, had taken Philadelphia. Cousin Owen heard that 1,600 British soldiers were camped west of the city. Sarah and her "delicate, chicken-hearted cousin" Liddy were scared. That night Sarah wrote that her family expected to be "in the midst of one Army or the other."

Surrounded by Soldiers

The farmhouse was quiet the next morning. A few neighbors passed by, taking wheat to grind at the flour mill down the road. At noon, Sarah was standing in the

Sarah Spoke "Plain" English

Sarah Wister and her family, like other Quakers, used words and expressions that were different from the way other colonists talked. As the English language changed, the Quakers continued speaking in "plain language."

More than a hundred years before Sarah was born, only people of high rank, like kings and queens, could be addressed as "you." Everyone else was referred to by the pronouns "thee" and "thou."

Gradually "thee" and "thou" became an old-fashioned way of speaking. Most people said "you," but the English Bible still kept "thee" and "thou." The Quakers decided to continue speaking in the biblical style.

Suddenly, four men rode up to the door.

kitchen. Suddenly, four men on horseback rode up to the door. Since they were dressed in blue-and-red uniforms, Sarah thought they were British soldiers. Horrified, she raced to the house. To her great relief, they were colonial soldiers who wanted to buy horses. Her father had no horses to sell, but he served them glasses of wine and they talked about the fighting. To Sarah's relief, the men "behaved very civil."

In the afternoon, the sky grew dark and stormy. The rain poured down in silver sheets. Wet leaves fell from the trees, leaving their branches bare. Sarah and her cousins stayed indoors by the fire, sewing and listening to her father talk about what General Washington would do. That night she climbed into bed. In the distance she could hear the clap of cannons. She fell asleep with their thunder in her ears.

The next morning, Sarah lay awake in bed thinking about her friends when cousin Liddy came running into the room.

"Sarah, get up," she cried. "Everyone is downstairs. Drums and fifes and wagons are rattling louder than we've ever heard!" Sarah dressed and ran downstairs. The grownups said Washington was marching closer. Mr. Wister was sure the American army would drive the British out of Philadelphia. Sarah and her younger sister were permitted to walk down the road to watch as Washington and his men passed by.

Sarah and her sister watched as Washington and his men passed by.

As Sarah and Betsy returned to the farmhouse, two officers rode up to the door and asked if they could have quarters for General Smallwood. Aunt Foulke said she had plenty of room for them. One of the officers dismounted and wrote "Smallwood's Quarters" over the door, to keep out straggling soldiers. Soon the house would be full of soldiers.

General Smallwood Arrives

Sarah and Betsy ran upstairs to change into clean dresses. Sarah brushed her blonde hair back and covered it with a fresh white cap. In the evening General Smallwood came with six attendants, a large guard of soldiers, a number of horses, and baggage wagons. The yard and house glittered with military equipment. Sarah loved the bustle and adventure. "There was great running up and down stairs," she wrote, "so I had an opportunity of seeing and being seen, the former most agreeable to be sure.

"Some of the officers supped with us. . . . They retired about ten. How new is our situation. I feel in good spirits although we are surrounded by an Army. The house is full of officers, yard alive with soldiers, very peaceable sort of men though, they eat like other folks, talk like them, and behave themselves with elegance, so I will not be afraid of them."

The American officers stayed at the farmhouse for two weeks while they made preparations for a winter camp. Sarah spent extra time dressing for dinner and looking her best. She wrote in her journal more often, too, sure that her friends Debby and Sally would love hearing about her new chintz dress and the handsome young officers who visited the farmhouse. Sarah and her cousins made friends with them. They drank tea together, and the soldiers talked about the families they left at home when they joined the war.

On the first of November, the army was ready to leave the farmhouse. Sarah wished the soldiers could stay. A page in her journal read:

"Today the Militia marches and the Genl and officers leave us high ho. I am very sorry, for when you have been with agreeable people tis impossible not to feel regret when they bid you adieu, perhaps forever. When they leave us we shall be immersed in solitude. About two o'clock the General and Major came to bid us adieu. They shook hands with Daddy and Mammy. Very friendly to us. They bowed politely. Our hearts were full.

"We stood at the door to take a last look, all of us very solemn. The major turned his horse's head, rode back, and dismounted. 'I have forgot my pistols,' he said. He ran up the stairs and came swiftly back as if wishing he could stay, but by duty he was compelled to go. He remounted his horse. 'Farewell, ladies, till I see you again.' He cantered away. We looked at him till the turn in the road hid him from our sight. I wonder whether we shall ever see him again. He has our wish for his safety."

The next day was one of the last times Sarah would write in her little journal for several months. Winter was coming. The colonial soldiers would soon be camped only a few miles away. The farmhouse was quiet once more. Sarah wished the soldiers had not gone. "It seems strange not to see our house as it used to be," she wrote. "We are very still, no rattling of Waggons or glittering of muskets. The beating of the distant drum is all we hear."

What Did Sarah Wear?

Quaker women wore bonnets, dresses, and shawls that were a soft gray, sometimes with a dainty white scarf long enough to be tucked in at the waist. They wore white aprons that covered their dresses while they worked. Quakers used hidden hooks to fasten their garments. To them, buttons and buckles were showy decorations. They believed it was better to dress and live as simply as possible.

Sarah Wister did not always wear gray. In her journal she described some of the dresses she wore when the soldiers visited. One of her favorites was long, with purple and white stripes, a white petticoat, and a muslin apron. A plain white cap usually covered her head. It kept her hair neat so she wouldn't spend time worrying about how she looked. Sarah believed it was better to devote her time to thinking about God.

Joseph Plumb Martin Goes to War

Grandfather took down his musket.

The following story is based upon the recollections of Joseph Plumb Martin, a fifteen-year-old Connecticut boy who lived with his grandparents until he joined the Continental army in 1776.

The morning sun streaked through the window of the keeping room. Grandfather and Grandmother Plumb were up early. They sat at the long pine table, finishing their breakfast tea. Young Joseph was still asleep in the little room upstairs. Good, Grandfather thought. The boy would be tired enough before this day ended. Wherever he lay his head tonight, Joseph would sleep soundly.

Grandfather rose from the table. The work today would be light. The season's hay was cut and stacked. In the garden were a few onions to pull and early peas to pick. But first he must collect the things Joseph would take.

From the narrow cupboard beside the buttery, Grandfather took down his musket and bayonet. The long musket was his prized possession. He had hunted many deer and ducks with this rifle. It would go with Joseph now, to fight the British. The shiny bayonet, too, would defend the boy at close range. On a shelf above the rifle was Grandfather's cartouche box, filled with lead shot and gunpowder. Joseph would need this.

As he gathered the weapons, Grandfather thought about Joseph's eagerness to enlist. Grandfather had not consented to it. The two had talked about this many times since spring, when Grandfather first "smelt the rat" of war. But Joseph had his own ideas. Two nights ago, he had stayed late in the village. When Grandfather saw him the next morning, the look on Joseph's face told all.

Joseph's Silver Dollar

Joseph Martin reported to the Connecticut army. A fellow who was recruited received a bounty, or reward, for signing up. Joseph was impressed when he received a silver dollar. As the war continued and more men were needed, they were also promised land.

Congress believed the war would be over quickly, so it passed a law that ordered all healthy males between sixteen and sixty years of age to serve a one-year enlistment.

"Well, you are a going soldiering then, are you?" Grandfather had asked him. Joseph said nothing. Grandfather Plumb put his own feelings aside. "I suppose you must be fitted out for the expedition, since it is so."

Now Grandfather went into the keeping room to help Grandmother prepare food for Joseph's knapsack. From a shelf in the buttery he took down a heavy wheel of cheese. As he cut a thick wedge, he heard footsteps on the stairs.

"Good morning, Grandfather," Joseph said, rubbing his eyes. He watched the old man put the cheese and a small loaf of bread into the knapsack. Joseph turned and saw Grandfather's musket resting against the wall. Joseph had wondered if he could take it, but he dared not ask.

"Morning, Joseph," Grandfather replied. He looked at his tall grandson. He and his wife had gladly raised their daughter's child for these nine years. Susanna and Ebenezer Martin, a preacher, had gone to Pennsylvania, leaving Joseph to be cared for by the Plumbs. With the boy away, too, Grandfather knew, the large house would be quieter than ever.

"You're a good marksman, Jos," Grandfather continued, glancing toward his bayonet and gun. "Best take those with you. You can't fight emptyhanded, and there's no certainty you'll get a musket when you report today." His voice grew stern. "I don't need to tell you how to care for it."

"No, Sir," Joseph answered in a strong voice. "I will take care of it, on my word."

Joseph ate his breakfast while Grandfather finished filling the knapsack. The day would be hot and he must leave soon. The walk to Milford was only a few miles, but he could not guess his journey beyond the village.

In his room Joseph dressed in his short, coarse jacket, trousers, and hunting boots. His extra shirt and pants were rolled into his sack. He straightened the quilts and tucked them neatly into the mattress. He shook out his pillow, wondering when he would sleep in his own bed again. His grandparents had loved and cared for him. He would miss them, especially Grandfather. But it was hard to say a thing like that.

An Army of Volunteers

When fighting began in 1776, each of the thirteen colonies already had its own militia, men who volunteered to fight when trouble broke out in their own towns and responded instantly to a village crisis.

Each colony gathered weapons and ammunition to be ready for a major emergency.

The new congress needed a "standing," or regular, army of trained Continental soldiers—not just to defend each colony, as the militia would still do—but to fight *wherever* battles took place.

Every new Continental soldier was assigned to a company of eighty-six men, who were commanded by four officers and four staff officers. Eight companies made up one regiment, also called a battalion.

In all, there were twenty-six regiments of foot soldiers or infantrymen, one regiment of riflemen, and one of artillerymen. "Light" troops were foot soldiers who explored the countryside first, mapping the way for the regular army to follow, and searching for enemies.

Joseph ate his breakfast while his Grandfather filled his knapsack.

"Joseph." Grandfather's voice called from below. Joseph raced down the stairs. Grandfather was standing in the parlor, holding his small pocket Bible. Joseph took it solemnly. He and Grandfather went back to the keeping room and packed the last of Joseph's things. It was time to leave.

They walked down the path from the house to the main road. Grandmother's eyes filled with tears as she hugged him. Grandfather turned to Joseph.

"God keep you safe, lad." He took Joseph's hand in his and gave it a warm shake.

Joseph straightened his shoulders. "I'll be home by Christmas Day, Grandfather," he said brightly. "Captain Peck promised."

OCTOBER 1776: Yankee Fleet Attacked. On October 11, the fleet of American Commander Benedict Arnold was nearly destroyed during a seven-hour attack on Lake Champlain. Two days later, after a second battle, Arnold's men escaped through fog, then beached and burned their ships so the British could not use them.

DECEMBER 25 and 26, 1776: Victory at Trenton. In a sneak night attack, Washington's men stole across the Delaware River and captured 2,000 British troops at dawn. Six Americans were killed in the one-hour battle.

"I'll be home by Christmas Day, Grandfather!"

NEW SHIRTS AND OLD WEAPONS

Most men who joined the army knew how to fire a rifle, and some were fine marksmen. Many were keen hunters who knew their way in the forest.

Each man was expected to bring his own weapon when he enlisted. But some did not own rifles or muskets. During the war the army constantly ran short of weapons and ammunition.

The army's first standard uniform was a fringed hunting shirt. General Washington liked it because it was cheap and easy to sew. It was cool in summer and by adding layers of underwear it was warm in winter. Most of all, Washington said, the enemy would see the armed rifleman in uniform and know he was looking at a true marksman.

For his men Washington ordered leather boots that had no left or right foot. They were identical. The soldier switched them every morning to assure even wearing. To look his best, he tried to keep them clean and blackened.

JANUARY 3, 1777: Second Victory for Washington. In a second stunning victory over the British, Washington's forces drove British troops north. Rebels began march to Morristown, New Jersey, to retire to winter quarters.

PLEASE PASS THE FLOUR

Keeping clean was one of the biggest challenges of the soldier's day. To wash, soldiers dug small "sinks" near a river, poured in a bucket of water, cleaned up as well as possible, and then filled the pit again with earth. The popular hairstyle for men was long hair, gathered into a "tail" at the neck, and whitened with powder. At the start of the war, officers dusted their hair with flour to get it white. This habit soon became impractical, and soldiers only powdered for a special occasion, such as the visit of a general.

pack

half gaiters

stockings

straight shoes
(No left or right.)

round hat

fringed linen
hunting dress

tomahawk

bayonet

cocked hat

crossed belts

white
waistcoat

brown bess
musket

white linen overalls

JULY 6, 1777: Ticonderoga Falls to British. After moving men south from Canada this month, General John Burgoyne captured the American fort at Ticonderoga, New York. Taken in the sweep were many weapons abandoned by retreating American general Arthur St. Clair.

twenty-four pounder cannon

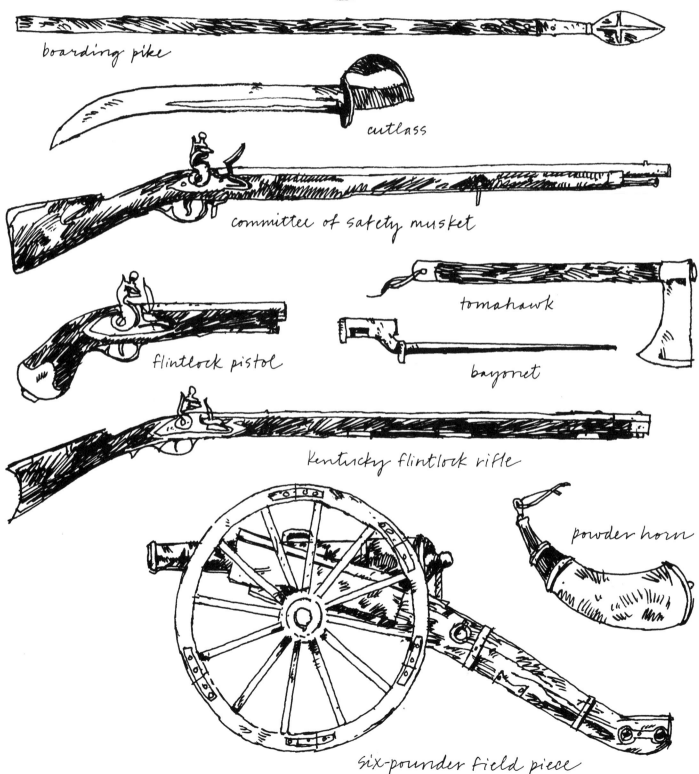

boarding pike

cutlass

committee of safety musket

flintlock pistol

tomahawk

bayonet

Kentucky flintlock rifle

powder horn

six-pounder field piece

One Hard Winter

He saw the snow stained from bleeding feet.

The British captured Philadelphia in September 1777. Congress told General Washington to keep his eye on the enemy. To do that, Washington would need shelter for eleven thousand soldiers. The canvas tents they slept in during the summer would not protect them from winter blizzards.

Eighteen miles northwest of Philadelphia, Valley Creek flowed through Quaker farm country. Stone houses dotted the valley. Beside the creek, a water wheel powered an iron forge, giving the land its name, Valley Forge. North of the forge, the creek flowed into the Schuylkill River. The land sloped south, making a perfect lookout. With farms to provide food, the forge to make weapons, and the hills for protection, Washington thought it would be the perfect spot.

As the first snows fell, General Washington drew his soldiers together for the final march to their new camp. Many of them had gone barefoot during the summer and autumn. But now, snow and freezing rain were falling hard. Wagon tracks along the muddy roads froze into sharp ruts. Soldiers who had no shoes wrapped their feet in old rags. Washington rode behind his men. He saw the blood-red snow, stained from torn and bleeding feet. He said nothing, but his heart grieved.

Night fell as the men entered the valley. Too tired to make camp, they dropped to sleep on the frozen earth. In the morning they began chopping logs to make shelters. They would build one thousand huts, or cabins. Each would be sixteen by fourteen feet, and hold twelve men. A door would open at one end, with a fireplace on the opposite wall.

Washington offered a prize of twelve dollars for the first cabin built. On the second night in camp, he awarded the money. The men had built their hut without nails. It had wood shingles. Mud filled the cracks between the logs. The dirt floor was damp, but they made simple stools to

SEPTEMBER 26, 1777: Philadelphia Falls to British!!! General Howe today entered colonial capital to capture the city. Congress fled to safety in Lancaster eight days ago. Fearing it would be melted down for British ammunition, the huge bell on the state house was removed by rebels and hidden in a church in Allentown.

sit on. If they were lucky, they would get clean hay to sleep on. Except for the stools and wall pegs to hold clothes, the huts had no furniture. All the soldiers needed now were food, clothing, blankets, and shoes.

In those days, fighting stopped during winter. "Gentlemen" did not fight in winter. But the soldiers were hardly living like gentlemen. Lice crawled on unwashed skin, spreading diseases. Death came often: typhoid fever and smallpox killed more than two thousand men.

Getting supplies to Valley Forge was almost impossible. Time and again, the food ran out. Thousands deserted at the first chance. Soldiers had to eat corn intended for the horses. They even ate leather from old boots.

With no meat, clothing, or shoes for his men, and temperatures below zero, Washington was desperate. He sent word to the congress that without money for supplies, his army would either "starve, dissolve, or disperse."

To save ammunition, the soldiers stopped firing their cannon as a wake-up call. Instead, they beat drums. They had orders not to shoot at birds or animals, even for food. During the worst times, breakfast, dinner, and supper were the same. The meal was a thick paste made of flour and water, cooked over an open flame. They called it "fire cake."

A SOLDIER'S IRON BONDAGE

Soldiers complained about having to carry cooking gear, "the most useless things in the army." When it was Joseph Martin's turn to carry the cast-iron kettle, he refused. "I was so beat out . . . with hunger and fatigue that I could hardly move one foot before the other. I told my messmates that I *could not* carry our kettle any farther. They said they *would* not carry it any farther. Of what use was it? They had nothing to cook."

Martin's arms were almost dislocated. He set the kettle down. One of his companions "gave it a shove with his foot and it rolled down against the fence, and that was the last I ever saw of it." The next morning, Martin saw that several other soldiers, too, had disobeyed orders and were "rid of their iron bondage."

OCTOBER 7, 1777: Burgoyne Surrenders!!!! In a stunning victory for rebels, General John Burgoyne surrendered at Saratoga, New York. Two major battles and thousands of casualties left British army weak. In surrender agreement, Burgoyne asked that 6,000 British prisoners be sent home with promise not to return and fight again.

"I could not carry our kettle any farther."

DECEMBER 1777: Washington at Valley Forge for Winter. American army under General Washington entered winter quarters at Valley Forge, Pennsylvania, outside Philadelphia. Troops severely short of all essential supplies.

A DOCTOR'S DIARY

A doctor, Albigence Waldo, kept a diary of his months at Valley Forge. He knew many men were worse off than he, but he was miserable:

"Dec 12th We are ordered to march over the river—it snows—I'm sick—eat nothing—no whiskey—no baggage. . . . Cold and uncomfortable. . . .

"Dec 14th Poor food—hard lodging—cold weather—fatigue—nasty clothes—nasty cookery—vomit half my time—smoked out of my senses . . . I can't endure it—why are we sent here to starve and freeze . . . a pox on my bad luck. Here comes a bowl of beef soup—full of burnt leaves and dirt, sickish enough to make a Hector spew—away with it, Boys—I'll live like the chameleon upon air.

"Dec 15th Quiet. Eat persimmons, found myself better for their lenient operation. . . .What have you for dinner boys? 'Nothing but fire cake & water, Sir.'—'Gentlemen, the supper is ready.' What is your supper, lads? 'Fire cake & water, Sir.'

"What have you got for breakfast, lads? 'Fire cake and water, Sir.'"

Washington took drastic action. He sent General Nathanael Greene through the countryside, to buy food and supplies. On February 26, Greene returned to Valley Forge, leading a caravan of wagons loaded with meat, vegetables, hay, salt, and honey. More officers followed, driving herds of cattle, sheep, and pigs. The worst was finally over for the courageous men who had survived that terrible winter.

JANUARY 29, 1778: Georgia Falls to British. After capturing Augusta and Savannah, Georgia, British called on southern loyalists to help seize remaining southern colonies.

FEBRUARY 6, 1778: Treaties Signed with France. Commissioner Benjamin Franklin and Count Vergennes met today in Paris to sign two treaties. Terms of first make them partners. Second states both will fight together until American independence is won.

For supper they had fire cake and water.

General in the Storm: A Game

Bitterly cold winds, freezing rain, and deep snow brought a halt to fighting in the northern colonies. Frozen weapons and wet ammunition would not work. On both sides, the generals took their men into "winter quarters." If they hadn't, this old game of military strategy might have become a real test of survival. Play it with a friend and see how well you would do if you were an American general lost in a snowstorm, in enemy territory.

What You Need:

Draw this game board on white cardboard or paper. Draw an 8-inch square and divide it into sixteen equal parts. Add the triangle at the top, dividing it with lines, as shown. Using another piece of cardboard, make seventeen "men" by tracing around a quarter and cutting out the pieces. Color sixteen of the circles red and one blue. (The blue one is the American general, surrounded by the British redcoats.)

How to Play:

One player has sixteen soldiers, the other has the general. Red pieces are placed on the game board on the dark outside circles. The blue general is placed in the center white circle. All the pieces move one point (a point is where two or more lines intersect) per play along any straight line, but only the general may enter the triangle "cave" at the top of the board. If he is trapped in the cave by the enemy soldiers, he loses the game.

The soldiers and the general capture each other in different ways. Soldiers capture the general by moving two men onto points on the same line, one on either side of him; this is called a *custodian* capture. The general captures two soldiers at once by moving to a point directly between two of them; this is called an *intervention* capture.

A soldier makes the first move. The game is over when the general is captured or trapped in the cave, or all the soldiers are captured.

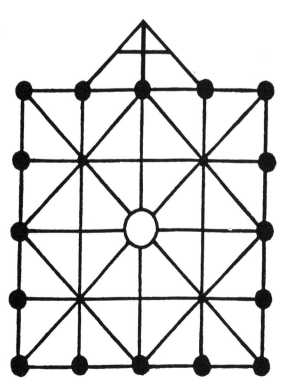

THE BRITISH MARCH TO NEW YORK

While Washington and his men camped in misery at Valley Forge, the British general William Howe enjoyed the comforts of city living only twenty miles away. But he never wanted war against the colonists, and he had said he would never fight against them. He asked permission to resign, naming many other reasons. In May 1778, the popular general returned to England.

The new British commander in Philadelphia, Sir Henry Clinton, had problems. He couldn't hold the city captive and still have enough men to fight Washington. He also heard rumors that the French army might join the war and help the colonists by keeping the British from their supplies in New York.

General Clinton decided to march to New York before it was too late. Somehow, he had to get his men and equipment out of Philadelphia. It wouldn't be easy. Many loyalist Philadelphians would follow the British army. They were afraid to be there when the rebel troops returned.

THE CONTINENTAL ARMY ATTACKS

When Washington learned the British had left Philadelphia on June 18, his army, now well trained and healthy, went after them. The temperature was nearly 100 degrees and it began raining. In their stylish uniforms, the ten thousand British soldiers were drenched and uncomfortable. Each dragged eighty pounds of stuff in a pack. Washington's men were light on their feet and ready to test themselves.

In ten days, the rebel army caught up with the British, near Monmouth, New Jersey. Washington had planned an attack, but instead, one of his officers ordered the men to retreat. When the general caught up with them, he was amazed to see them marching *away* from the British! Witnesses said their commander in chief lost his temper and "swore till the leaves shook on the trees."

Washington took control. In a fierce battle, nearly four hundred men were killed on each side, and many died of sunstroke. During the night, the British escaped to safety in New York. The Battle of Monmouth was considered a tie, but it was a good test for the soldiers from Valley Forge. It proved they could fight after all.

THE SOUP THAT WON THE WAR

The official cook of the Continental army came from Philadelphia. He was a German named Christopher Ludwick. Ludwick was a soldier whose main job was to feed the men. He never had enough of the right ingredients, but he would experiment with anything.

Ludwick created a new supper for the hungry troops at Valley Forge. He had very little food but he knew the soldiers must have something warm and filling. According to legend, Ludwick combined tripe (stomach lining) and other animal insides, peppers, and spices to make a soup. To disguise the taste of the meat, which was probably not fresh, he added hot red pepper and black peppercorns.

Ludwick named his soup "Philadelphia Pepper Pot." He served it one freezing night when the soldiers were near starvation. Hot and spicy, the Pepper Pot soup filled them up and lifted their spirits. Some people still claim it was this soup that really won the war!

Philadelphia Pepper Pot

1 lb. ground beef or chuck
2 large sliced onions
2 celery sticks, chopped
4 potatoes, chopped
4 carrots, sliced
herbs: 2 tsp. each dried parsley and marjoram, ½ tsp. dried thyme, ⅛ tsp. crushed red pepper (more if you want fire!), ½ tsp. allspice, 3 whole cloves, salt, and lots of coarse black pepper.

1. Brown ground beef and onions in large kettle. Add ½ gallon of water, carrots, potatoes, and all seasonings.

2. Bring soup to boil and then reduce heat to medium low and cook 20 minutes, until carrots and potatoes are tender. Serve hot.

MARCH 13, 1778: England Declares War on France. News of French and American alliance has reached England. Angered by the treaty, England has declared war on longtime enemy France.

APRIL 24, 1778: Jones Captures *Drake*. In a feat of daring, Captain John Paul Jones captured the British warship *Drake*, killing the captain and forty British sailors. Jones has spent past two years raiding and capturing ships along English coast, with congressional permission. *Drake* is now largest man-of-war captured by Americans.

America's First Flags

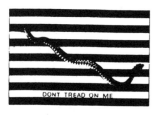

From top: Britain's Union Jack was in the corner of the first national American flag; the first Stars and Stripes, 1777; the flag of Bunker Hill; flag flown by Washington's squadron, 1775; Rhode Island's flag included a rattlesnake; the "New Constellation of Stars" flag, 1777.

It's difficult to trace the creator of America's first flag because *everyone* loved flags, made them, and flew them. The "Union Jack," Great Britain's flag, was a popular model for colonies that adopted flags. Designers shrank the criss-crossed red, white, and blue British design, and moved it to the upper left corner. Red and white stripes representing the first American colonies filled the body of the flag.

As the colonies moved toward independence, flag designs became more unique and creative. They were decorated with everything from stars, stripes, and slogans, to snakes.

Snakes?

Rhode Island designed a rattlesnake flag that warned the British, "Don't Tread on Me." South Carolina flew a rattlesnake flag, too, but skipped the words. The coiled rattler on a bright yellow background said it all.

As fighting began, Revolutionary War flags carried military designs. One had a burgundy background and a soldier pointing a rifle. Beneath it were the now-familiar words of the Revolution, "Liberty or Death."

The flag to remember the Battle of Bunker Hill had a simple design. The background was blue. In the upper left corner was a square of white, a red cross, and a green pine tree.

Rhode Island's snake flag was replaced as the colony became optimistic about winning the conflict. The new flag was white, with thirteen stars on a blue corner border. In the center of the flag was a blue ship's anchor. A banner above the anchor said "Hope."

We'd Rather Do It Ourselves

Even France designed an American flag for the colonies, adding a familiar French motif, a white *fleur de lis*, at the top and twelve stars below it.

Eagles on flags were almost as popular as stars. General Philip Schuyler requested a silk flag with an eagle and thirteen stars in the upper corner, and thirteen stripes in the body of the flag. This is one of the first known examples of the combination of thirteen stars and stripes.

The Official American Flag

The Flag Act of June 14, 1777, called for the new American flag to carry a circle of thirteen stars on a body of thirteen red and white stripes. It became the official symbol of the new United States, and remained so until 1795, when two more stars and stripes were needed to represent two new states, Kentucky and Vermont. The original Stars and Stripes remained popular long after it was officially outdated.

THE MYSTERY OF THE FIRST FLAG

Betsy Ross is famous for stitching the first American flag. According to legend, in 1776 General Washington paid a visit to the Philadelphia upholstery shop of Elizabeth ("Betsy") Ross, a widowed seamstress.

Betsy's grandson said he heard the family story when he was about five years old. He heard that the general and Betsy sat in the parlor drawing sketches and talking about what that first official flag should look like.

The Ross family also has some old letters that describe Washington's visit to Betsy. She said she would "try" to make it. This is the only evidence that Betsy Ross might have sewed the flag. As for proof of this story, however, there is none.

It is true that Betsy Ross was a seamstress and she made several flags, so she could have made the official American flag. But another version of the story claims that she was wealthy and would have given the flag project to one of her employees.

The honor of making the first flag *could* belong to a forgotten seamstress or tailor. The truth may never be known.

who really made the first stars and stripes?

JUNE 21, 1779: Spain Enters War. Britain refused to give Spain land as reward for not fighting in war. In response, Spain declared war on Great Britain, but refused to support America's independence or offer military assistance.

Design Your Flag

A flag is the *symbol* of an important idea. What idea would you make into a flag for you? What symbol could stand for your school? Could you create a symbol for African Americans? Or Native Americans? How about a flag to stand for kids everywhere?

Draw your flag on a large sheet of construction paper. When it's finished, see if you can adapt it to cloth and sew it.

① DRAW YOUR IDEA FIRST ON PAPER TO MAKE A PATTERN.

② CUT PATTERN SHAPES FROM PAPER OR CLOTH.

③ SEW PIECES ONTO A BACKGROUND CLOTH.

THE BRITISH PLAN FOR VICTORY

The British were alarmed when they discovered the conflict in Boston was only the start of rebellion spreading through *all* the colonies. In 1777 General John Burgoyne (rhymes with "her coin") made a plan to bring the disobedient colonies under control. It had three parts. Parliament approved it.

Soldiers from the North

First, Burgoyne would lead a large army into Canada. He would recruit Canadians and Indians, and march south to Albany, New York, an important colonial city on the Hudson River. Another British army would sweep north through the colonies and meet Burgoyne and his soldiers at the river. A third force would move toward Albany from the Mohawk River region to the west.

Once the British had control of the Hudson River Valley, the six New England colonies (Maine, New Hampshire, Vermont, Massachusetts, Rhode Island, and Connecticut) would be isolated from New York. Unable to receive shipments of food and supplies from New York, the northern colonies would grow desperate.

A March from the South

In the second part of the British plan, soldiers would also march north from East Florida, and overrun the southern colonies. On their way, they expected thousands of loyal colonists, especially in Georgia and South Carolina, to join them in the fight to continue British rule.

The strong British navy would also take control of the southern seacoast. Without shipments of food from other parts of the world, the south could not survive. When Burgoyne planned this strategy, the colonies didn't even *have* a navy that could protect their seaports.

Capture New York for a Base

The third part of the plan was to capture the New York settlement at the mouth of the Hudson River. New York Harbor was the heart of the colonial shipping trade. When the British captured it, Burgoyne thought, the rebellious little cluster of colonies would think twice about independence. The British planned to make New York their base of operations during the war.

Burgoyne's plan was good for many reasons. The colonies were not well organized or cooperative with each other. Their little militias were no match for the British army, the most powerful in the world. And the colonies had almost no money. How could they possibly buy war supplies?

The British were confident that this three-part war plan would succeed and the colonies would surrender. They did not expect a serious fight. But they misjudged many things. They did not see how angry the colonists were. They underestimated the skill of the ordinary colonist, who was a marksman with a rifle and knew his way through the fields and forests of America. The British missed other clues, too. They did not allow for human mistakes in their own plans. Most of all, they did not know how many colonists would willingly *die* to win independence.

Pirates for Hire

Israel wanted badly to go ashore.

Privateer Wages

In 1779, a fourteen-year-old cabin boy's portion of the prizes, after a single month at sea, was $700, one ton of sugar, thirty-five gallons of rum, and twenty pounds apiece of cotton, ginger, logwood, and allspice.

The higher the rank, the greater portion of the prize received. One admiral received $122,697. The greatest share of the prize went to the owner of the ship.

Israel Trask climbed the ladder to the deck. He was glad to be out of the hot smoke of the galley even for a few minutes. He leaned against the ship's rail, smelled the fresh salty air, and gazed across the harbor at the village. Above the creaking of the ship's rigging, he heard a barking dog and distant voices as people made their way home for the evening. Windows glowed as lamps were lit one by one. It was almost dark.

Israel was a cabin boy and cook's helper. His ship, the *Black Prince*, had anchored at Townsend, Massachusetts, several days before, after a long voyage from Ireland. Israel wanted badly to go ashore just for the change. But he could not. The owner had ordered the ship to sail north to the Penobscot River with ships of the Continental navy to raid the British there. They would leave Townsend the next morning on the outgoing tide.

Such was life on a privateer. There was no money to be made in a friendly port. Privateers like the *Black Prince* were ships for hire. Their pay was the cargo and money they took from ships they raided. The Continental Congress had hired the *Black Prince* to capture the British ships at the mouth of the Penobscot River.

Israel had volunteered to be a privateer when he was twelve years old, after serving in his father's regiment as a cook and messenger. When his father became ill, Israel quit the regiment to become a privateer. His father knew there was money to be made at sea.

His father was right. In the two trips Israel completed as a privateer, his share of the captured cargo and money was many times more than his pay as a soldier.

Israel took one last look at the evening sky. It had been another long day. He had risen to help the cook with breakfast at 5 A.M. and his duties were still not finished. He went below to the crew's sleeping quarters. The air was damp and smelled of sweat.

Israel began undoing the netting that stored the hammocks. Soon hammocks were everywhere. They were spaced so closely that a person had no choice when he got in his hammock but to lie still. Israel made sure each hammock had a blanket. Then he climbed into his hammock, yawned once, and fell fast asleep.

To Penobscot Bay: Summer 1779

Daybreak. The tide has turned. The anchor is up. The *Black Prince* is on its way, along with three warships, the *Tyrannicide, Hazard,* and *Active,* twenty-two transport ships carrying several thousand troops, and sixteen other privateer ships.

Israel feels uneasy. This new mission is different than the other two he has been on.

"I don't like it, Boy," says the cook. He picks up a sack of flour and pours the contents into a cast-iron pot. "There won't be a prize to share out of this one. I can feel it in my bones. It's all trouble and no money."

Israel pours a bucket of water into the pot and begins to stir the biscuit mixture. "Will there be any fighting?"

"I pray not, but I fear so," says the cook.

The British are building a fort at the mouth of the Penobscot River. If they are allowed to complete it, the coasts of the Massachusetts and New Hampshire colonies will never be safe. Fighting is certain.

For four days the ships follow the rocky New England coast north. On the fifth day they reach their destination in high winds and choppy water. In the distance the fort, missing one wall, can be seen atop a steep bank. British warships are anchored near the fort. They raise their anchors. On land the alarm is sounded.

General Solomon Lovell is in command of all the Continental forces. Paul Revere is in charge of artillery. The most powerful warship in the Continental navy, the *Warren,* is commanded by Captain Dudley Saltonstall.

The *Warren* moves in. The British on shore fire their cannon at the *Warren* below.

Aboard a Privateer

Life on board a privateer ship was no picnic. The drinking water was so muddy you could not see the bottom of your cup. The food never varied. It was always terrible. Biscuits were moldy, overcooked if you were lucky. The pork was heavily salted and often spoiled. Vegetables consisted of dried peas and maybe potatoes. Lack of fresh vegetables and fruit brought on scurvy, a disease which caused gums to bleed and teeth to fall out. At sea, work was always the same and never ending. There were sails to be hoisted, rigging to be manned, repairs to be made, food to be cooked, and watches to be taken—to keep an eye out for enemy vessels. And at the end of a long day there was sleep in dim, crowded, smelly quarters. It was worse in the British navy. Conditions were just as bad, but discipline was more harsh.

The British fire their cannon at the *Warren*.

The British warships fire their cannon as well. The *Warren* returns fire. Sea water explodes into the air. Gunsmoke turns the sky and sea gray. The gun and cannon fire accomplishes nothing. No ships are damaged on either side. Cannonballs hit the steep banks, but miss the fort.

Israel watches, thinking the "prize" on this journey will be getting away with his life.

Panic Sets In

Captain Saltonstall's officers urge him to attack the fort. He refuses. Instead he sends men out to watch the British activities.

A party of marines, volunteers, and artillery is sent ashore while ships fire upon the British fort and their warships. The rebel marines climb the steep bank toward the fort, digging their fingers into the dirt, holding onto bushes and trees. They get within six hundred yards of the fort.

There they stop. General Lovell will not order his troops to attack the fort until Captain Saltonstall has destroyed all British warships. Saltonstall refuses! Until the fort has been captured, he will not risk his ships. The privateer captains agree with Saltonstall.

The mission is stalled. The rebel soldiers near the fort retreat to their ships. Thousands of men and forty-one ships wait for Captain Saltonstall to change his mind. And while they are waiting, panic sets in. Everyone knows that sooner or later the British will send reinforcements.

"We should pull up anchor and get out of here. That's what I say," the cook warns Israel.

"We can't do that," scolds Israel.

"No, Boy, we can't," replies the cook, "but we ought to. Mark my words."

A Just Prize

Captain Saltonstall lived through the disaster at Penobscot Bay. Since it was a disaster he created, he was court-martialed and thrown out of the navy for his refusal to cooperate with his commanding officer General Lovell.

Soon the ships are in flames.

The cook is correct. British reinforcements are on the way. Meantime, both sides continue firing at each other without any effect.

Two weeks later British warships reach Penobscot Bay. The rebel ships are easy targets for the British gunners. The British commanders do not hesitate. They attack. Cannonballs smash into the rebel ships.

The rebels sail up the Penobscot River. The British warships chase them. Saltonstall orders a flag raised, signalling his captains to set their ships on fire rather than let the British capture them.

Soon the ships are in flames. A cannonball blasts into the side of the *Black Prince*. Kegs of gunpowder explode. Men trample each other as they try to get off the ship. Israel is among those below deck trying to escape.

Israel spots a hole in the ship's hull, just above the line of the water. He squeezes through, holding onto his pack. The water is cold. Pieces of wood and dead bodies are floating all around. Israel and the other survivors swim to shore. Exhausted, they look back at the disaster behind them. They begin walking. Israel's destination is home: three hundred miles south.

Israel Trask later wrote about his ordeal, "I escaped to the dense forests and traveled through the wilderness about three hundred miles, with a pack on my shoulders containing a light blanket, a small piece of rusty pork, a few biscuits, a bottle of wine and one shirt. Wandering my way across streams through under brush, until the second day's march my shoes gave way. The rest of the way I performed on my bare feet, until I reached home."

Israel Trask was lucky. Five hundred men lost their lives and thirty-eight ships were sunk at Penobscot Bay. The British lost only fifteen men. It was the worst defeat in the Revolutionary War for the Continental navy.

What Became of Israel Trask

A month after returning home from his dangerous service on the *Black Prince*, Israel volunteered on the *Rambler*. He served as a privateer on six other vessels until 1782. He collected many prizes and was captured twice. After the war, he returned to Gloucester, Massachusetts, where he lived to the age of eighty.

NOTHING BUT PIRATES

Those serving in the regular Continental navy felt privateers were nothing more than hired pirates. Privateers were able fighters, but it was no secret that they would rather meet an unarmed British vessel filled with rich cargo than fight a warship with sixty guns.

Why did the Continental Congress enlist privateers? It had no choice. The Continental navy had only a few ships. By adding cannons to privately owned ships, a larger navy could be created instantly.

But the owners of the privateer ships wanted to keep everything they found on the ships they captured. The congress agreed. This enraged the crews on Continental navy ships, who were allowed to keep only 50 percent of the cargo they captured.

Besides, a sailor's pay was only eight dollars a month. A privateer's starting pay was twelve to sixteen dollars a month. It is not surprising that the congress had a very difficult time finding men to join the regular navy. Many of the sailors they found were British deserters. Some were prisoners who would rather sail than be locked up.

JULY 16, 1779: British Tromped in New York. Twelve hundred light infantry under General Anthony Wayne surprised British at Stony Point, New York. Seven hundred prisoners taken.

AUGUST 19, 1779: Lee Storms New Jersey. Major Henry Lee stormed Paulus Hook, New Jersey, clearing remaining British troops from area. British troops badly weakened, unlikely to fight again in north.

The Amazing "Turtle"

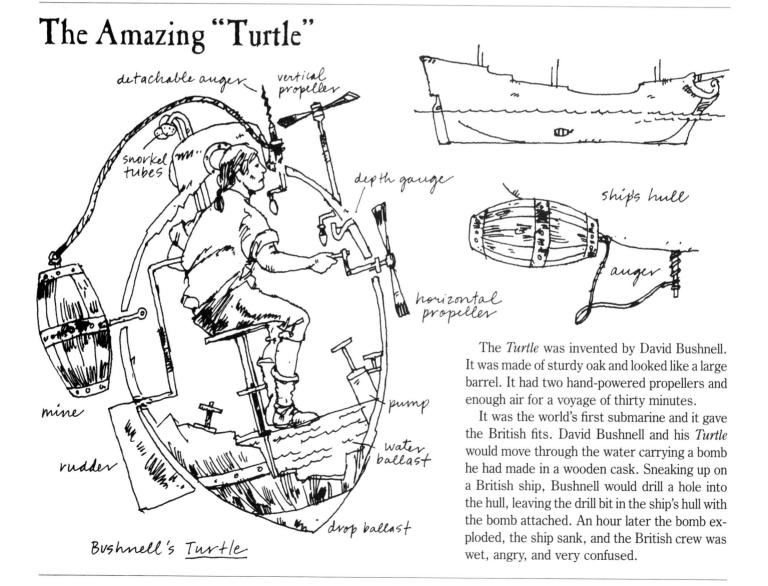

detachable auger   vertical propeller

snorkel tubes

depth gauge

ship's hull

horizontal propeller

auger

mine

pump

water ballast

rudder

drop ballast

Bushnell's Turtle

The *Turtle* was invented by David Bushnell. It was made of sturdy oak and looked like a large barrel. It had two hand-powered propellers and enough air for a voyage of thirty minutes.

It was the world's first submarine and it gave the British fits. David Bushnell and his *Turtle* would move through the water carrying a bomb he had made in a wooden cask. Sneaking up on a British ship, Bushnell would drill a hole into the hull, leaving the drill bit in the ship's hull with the bomb attached. An hour later the bomb exploded, the ship sank, and the British crew was wet, angry, and very confused.

Women in Battle

She stayed beside him, loading and firing his cannon.

Patriot women who stayed home during the war boycotted, or gave up, some products imported from England. They stopped drinking English tea and sewing their clothing from British wool. When the American armies marched past their houses, women tried to cook enough food for all the hungry soldiers.

Wherever battles took place, women were there to help, too. They took care of the wounded, hauled drinking water from creeks, fixed meals, and washed and mended clothing.

General Washington could not decide what to do about women who helped. He did not want them in danger, but they helped save lives and freed extra men for fighting. Among the colonists, for every one hundred men on the battlefields, nearly seven women helped nearby.

Mary Hayes followed her husband when he enlisted as an infantryman. She spent the winter at Valley Forge. She carried water for his gun crew at the Battle of Monmouth, where soldiers nicknamed her "Molly Pitcher." When her husband was hit, she stayed beside him, loading and firing his cannon. In 1832, Pennsylvania recognized her as a veteran and awarded her a pension.

Deborah Sampson was another daring young woman. She changed her name, cut her hair short, and disguised herself in a soldier's uniform. Deborah fought for nearly two years, until she was hit in the shoulder by a musket ball. People heard later that a woman had joined the army and pretended to be a man. Many of them could hardly believe such a shocking thing. Deborah, too, received veteran's benefits for her military service to the new United States.

SEPTEMBER 1779: Spain Takes British Ports. Spanish governor of Louisiana and his army captured British seaports in Spanish territory, including Baton Rouge, Natchez, and Manhac. Seizure marks first victory since Spain declared war on England in June.

MAY 12, 1780: Lincoln Surrenders. Americans witnessed worst defeat of war at Charleston, South Carolina, when General Benjamin Lincoln surrendered to British. Two hundred fifty-five redcoats killed. Cornwallis captured 5,400 American prisoners, four ships, and large supply of weapons. Lincoln was refused right to march with American flag flying or to play military music at surrender ceremony.

Victory at Yorktown

The men set to work building the base.

In the spring of 1781, the British ordered General Cornwallis to build a base for the Royal Navy at a town along the Virginia coast. Cornwallis had given up plans to take South Carolina and then North Carolina. Each small British victory in the south left him with fewer men.

Cornwallis hoped to catch General Lafayette and destroy patriot weapon stores. Soon two other British armies joined him. Together they made a force of seven thousand men.

Nearly every day Cornwallis received another letter from General Clinton in New York, changing instructions. Cornwallis was frustrated. To stop and fight Lafayette would look like disobeying orders. He marched his men north to the coast, toward Yorktown, Virginia, a small settlement on the York River, near the mouth of the Chesapeake Bay.

The men set to work building the base. Surrounded by swamps and low hills, their site was relatively well protected. Only a mile across the river was the town of Gloucester. British reinforcements were expected to sail into the river any day now. The British navy, too, was anchored off the coast. If he should ever need an escape route, Cornwallis thought, the ships were close enough to provide safety for his men.

MARCH 1781: Victory and Retreat. General Cornwallis dealt a crushing blow to American troops at the Battle of Guilford Courthouse in North Carolina. But British losses were so high Cornwallis dropped plans to retake the Carolinas. He is reported retreating to Wilmington to await reinforcements.

In early October, as Cornwallis built his Yorktown base, General Washington received the message that French ships were sailing toward the Chesapeake. He was pleased. Of course he would be there to offer Commander De Grasse, of the French navy, a proper welcome. Washington and his men marched to Yorktown. Lafayette's troops, too, arrived from the south. There were nearly sixteen thousand Continentals facing the British.

General Cornwallis found himself surrounded and outnumbered. He had thousands of sick, wounded, and hungry men, and winter was coming. He needed supplies. He had been told that the British navy was on its way with more troops, but no one knew when it might arrive. Cornwallis wrote to one of the British generals to say, "If you cannot relieve me very soon, you must be prepared to hear the very worst."

He was more alarmed when he learned that the French navy had arrived. Their ships blocked the bay. It was too late for the British navy to help now. Cornwallis had one last hope. During the night of October 16, he tried to get his men across the York River. If even three hundred of them could get through to General Clinton in New York, surely the general would find a way to send help.

As darkness fell, British soldiers climbed into boats and slipped across the water. Some made it safely to the other side. But clouds piled up, the wind roared in, and a ferocious storm lashed the water. The men could not see through sheets of rain, and the rough water tossed their boats like toys. Cornwallis called them back. He sent men to rescue those who were stranded on the opposite shore. As morning dawned, Cornwallis faced the grim truth. Surrender was his only choice.

JAMES ARMISTEAD LAFAYETTE

Everyone loved the Marquis de Lafayette for coming to help the desperate colonies fight England. History remembers a man from Virginia who was especially proud of serving under Lafayette.

James Armistead was a black slave. In March 1781, his master gave him permission to leave New Kent County, Virginia, when Lafayette marched to Williamsburg.

Lafayette, like any officer, could always use a good spy or two. James Armistead knew the Virginia countryside well and volunteered to help Lafayette in any way he could. To show his loyalty and prove his respect, James Armistead took a new last name: Lafayette.

The French general sent James Armistead Lafayette to Portsmouth to deliver secret messages and return with stolen information.

After seven months of working for Lafayette,

SEPTEMBER 1781: French Fleet Whips British in Chesapeake. Ships under French Count de Grasse and British Admiral Thomas Graves clashed off Yorktown coast. Victorious Grasse sailed up Chesapeake Bay to collect troops with Washington and Rochambeau. Three American armies already near Yorktown under Generals Lafayette, Wayne, and Von Steuben. Reinforcements bring Continental troops to 16,000.

OCTOBER 19, 1781: Cornwallis Surrenders. General Cornwallis surrendered to Americans at Yorktown. After rousing battlefield ceremony, British abandoned hopes of victory in America. Clinton arrived from New York, but quickly fled. Eight thousand British prisoners taken into custody.

James witnessed the British surrender at Yorktown. Imagine the surprise on the face of General Cornwallis when he stopped at American headquarters to bid farewell to Lafayette.

Cornwallis was shocked to find a black soldier (probably James) in the general's tent. Cornwallis quickly realized that James Lafayette had tricked the British, by counterspying for Lafayette! All the time, the British had been paying James to spy on the *Americans*!

General Lafayette reported that the black man "properly acquitted himself with some important communication I gave him . . . his intelligence from the enemy's camp were industriously collected and more faithfully delivered."

When they heard Lafayette's praise of this black spy, the Virginia government rewarded James Armistead Lafayette with freedom.

James Armistead Lafayette

The Youngest Major General

He was nineteen, he was French, he was the youngest major general in the war, and he had eight names! Marie Joseph Paul Yves Roch Gilbert du Motier, Marquis de Lafayette left France in 1777 to help the colonists fight against the British. He bought a commission as major general but was not given command of any troops until he had distinguished himself as George Washington's aide. He was an excellent commander who treated his soldiers with kindness and respect, and his successes encouraged France to officially enter the war on the side of the colonies. He was so popular in America that after the war, many of the new states made him an honorary citizen.

The World Turned Upside Down

October 18, 1781, dawned bright and clear after the night's violent downpour. Dressed in their smart new French-tailored uniforms of blue and brown, American soldiers shattered the morning stillness with the thunder of a hundred guns and cannon. The ground rumbled. Now and then, a shot fired back from the British line.

Through the drifting gunsmoke, a ragged drummer boy appeared on the horizon, walking down the slope toward them. He was followed by a British officer, waving a white handkerchief. All gunfire ceased as the American troops stared at the sight. Rushing forward, one of Washington's officers blindfolded the enemy officer and sent the drummer back across the lines. The officer was led to Washington's headquarters.

Washington unfolded the letter from General Cornwallis and read it slowly. He was relieved to end the bloodshed, but the British general's request surprised him. Cornwallis's letter described the ceremony the British would like: his army would march out proudly, carrying the British flag, beating the drums, as the band played. Cornwallis must have this one concession. Instead of prison, the letter continued, his men must be returned to Great Britain.

Washington could not agree to these terms. His reply to Cornwallis was that he was glad to spare further bloodshed, but he must think of the nation and not the man. The new prisoners could not sail home. There could be music later, but not as the British marched out. Nor would the British flag be flown. Washington remembered the American surrender at Charleston that June. The British had refused then to let General Benjamin Lincoln fly the Stars and Stripes or march to drums. Officers from both armies spent until midnight completing the conditions of surrender.

American soldiers spent the next morning lounging on the field, playing their fifes; the French were drumming and the British were blowing their bagpipes. At two o'clock in the afternoon of October 19, 1781, it was time. Lord Cornwallis sent a message. He was ill and could not attend.

Mounted on their horses, French soldiers made a wide circle on the field. A column of eight thousand British soldiers appeared on Hampton Road, marching in new red uniforms. They had not worn these in battle, and they would not give them up after the war. They marched past fourteen thousand troops—the French, in quiet rows in their handsome white uniforms, a line of white French flags fluttering in the wind, and the Americans. The Americans noticed that the British would look only at the French, not at them.

One by one, the defeated soldiers approached the center of the field. Some men sobbing, some in anger, they piled their rifles and muskets in the center of the field. The mound of weapons grew as the defeated soldiers circled and left the field.

Brigadier General Charles O'Hara replaced General Cornwallis at the symbolic exchange of the sword. He rode forward on his horse, ready to hand his weapon to the French Compte de Rochambeau. Rochambeau refused it. The Americans had won this war. The British could not surrender to the French.

"We are subordinates to the Americans," Rochambeau told O'Hara. "General Washington will give you your orders." O'Hara turned toward the victorious American general. Washington, too, refused the sword. O'Hara could not present it to the commanding general. He must offer it to an officer of a rank equal to his own. General Benjamin Lincoln extended his hand to accept the British sword. He tapped it in acceptance of surrender.

On the field, British drums beat sadly as the fifes played a mournful tune, "The World Turned Upside Down." Soldiers of four nations left the field as the fifes faded into silence. The world would never be the same.

If You Want to Know More

There are many stories to tell about the American Revolutionary War. We could only tell a few of them in this book. If you would like to know more, please read through this section. We have listed some of the books, videos, and historical sites that we thought might interest you.

Books

Who is the most interesting person you met in this book? You know that books about the lives of famous people are kept in the *biography* section of the library. Did you wonder how the Marquis de Lafayette got so rich, and what happened to him after the American Revolution? Then you'll enjoy *Lafayette: Man in the Middle*, by Sabra Holbrook (Atheneum, 1977).

Would you like to read the rest of Sarah Wister's diary, or find out what books *she* was reading at your age? Ask your librarian to find *The Journal and Occasional Writings of Sarah Wister*, edited and with an introduction by Kathryn Zabelle Derounian (Cranbury, New Jersey: Associated University Presses, Inc., 1987).

In 1773, Johnny Tremain was about your age. He was a smart, sassy Boston lad, bound to a silversmith and already good at making beautiful silverware. When he maimed his hand in an accident, he had to begin a new life. He walked the streets, looking for work. What he found was a wild horse to ride and a chance to serve the people of Boston. *Johnny Tremain*, by Esther Forbes Hoskins (Houghton Mifflin, 1943), is a book you won't be able to put down.

April Morning, another tale of the Revolution, takes you through one day with fifteen-year-old Adam Cooper. He's sick of his father's gruff ways and he's tired of being treated without respect. A neighbor drops in at suppertime to report that the men are meeting at the church later that night. Before dessert, Adam's mind is made up. He's thinking for himself from now on, whippings or not. Written by Howard Fast (Crown, 1961), the book takes you to the beginning of the Revolution, and the end of Adam's childhood.

If shipwrecks interest you, you'll want to know about an American ship, the *Defense*, that was blown up by the British in 1779. Scientists who study oceans—oceanographers—discovered it buried on the bottom of Penobscot Bay almost two hundred years later. For five years, divers worked to recover things from the ship. They found wooden plates, spoons, barrels of salted meat, leather boots, and pieces of weaponry. You can read the amazing story of how the *Defense* sank and was found again in *The Excavation of a Revolutionary War Privateer*, by Barbara Ford and David Switzer (William Morrow and Company, 1982).

Do you know what makes fireworks explode into different colors? Did you know that long ago, "wild men" were in charge of keeping crowds back from the fireworks so no one got burned? You'll find these and other facts about the Fourth of July in *Fireworks, Picnics, and Flags*, by James Cross Giblin (Clarion Books, 1983).

Maybe you'd like to read a little more about the *whole* war. In that case, get *The American Revolution*, by Richard B. Morris (Lerner Publications, 1985). It's a good, short book filled with other stories about the main events of the war.

Videos

Like books, television movies and videos about history can set your imagination on fire. You can watch the redcoats surrender, hear the congress at Philadelphia, ride with Revere, or sail the seas with John Paul Jones. The biggest challenge you face is not making the popcorn, but finding out who owns these movies, and how you can borrow them.

Dozens of movies about the Revolution have been made for school audiences. Your school district probably has some of them. Ask if there is a list of the movies your district owns, and if you can borrow them overnight or watch them after school.

Public libraries own or have access to movies and videos, too. Every library system is different. Talk with the people in charge at your public library. Tell them you'd like to know what they have or what they can order for you. In some states you can borrow materials from other city or county libraries, too.

Two excellent movies made from books named above are *Johnny Tremain* (Disney, 1957) and *April Morning*, made for television in 1988. Watch for *April Morning* in the weekly television listings, and tape it when it's shown next time.

Remember Deborah Sampson, the young woman who cut her hair and fooled everyone by wearing a man's uniform? *Deborah Sampson* (1976) tells you the whole story.

Everyone in the colonies was deeply affected by the war. In *The Americans, 1776* (1974), you'll meet a young woman who smuggled war secrets to General Washington, a family who remained loyal to the king, and many others who were torn by indecision about what to do.

Crafts and Projects

You can follow in Dr. Franklin's footsteps and try some *safe* electrical experiments and other science activities that are explained in *Electricity Experiments for Children*, by Gabriel Ruben (Dover, 1968), and *Science for You: 112 Illustrated Experiments*, by Bob Brown (Tab, 1988).

You and your friends could write a play about one of the dramatic events of the Revolution. For making costumes, get *Children's Costume in America, 1607–1910*, by Estelle Worrell (Scribner, 1980).

History Sites

History is all around you. Maybe the Revolution wasn't fought in your backyard, but do you know how old your town is, or who started it? Think about these questions and the ones that follow, and see if you can find the answers to them. When you've got them, quiz your parents to see how much they know about local history.

How did the town you live in get its name? Did Native Americans live there before other people came? Are any of their descendants still in the community?

Where are the oldest house and building in town? Visit the cemetery and find the oldest headstone there. Can you find a grave that dates from the Revolutionary War?

Ask your librarian if anyone in your community has written your town's history. See if you can call them, and if they have old photographs that show the town long ago. Ask them if they can tell you what the children did for fun back then. Find out how they discover things about the past. Maybe your town historian needs an assistant, and maybe that person can be *you*.

Do you live in one of the thirteen colonies? If so, you'll find the Revolutionary War monuments and markers in every direction. If you live a long way from the original colonies, plan an imaginary history escape to one of the landmark towns or battlefields described in this book.

Begin by choosing where you want to visit. Is it Valley Forge or Philadelphia, Pennsylvania; Yorktown, Virginia; Concord or Boston, Massachusetts; or someplace else? Go to the library and get travel books that include historical tours. (Most of the famous history sites are managed by the National Parks. In addition to tours, they often have special events during the year.) When you find the address of the place you want to visit, write to them for information. Get a road map and plan your route, or talk to a travel agent and plan an imaginary airline flight. As you gather your information, keep it in a safe place. Before you know it, your fantasy vacation might become a family reality.

To help you get started, here are a few of the most popular (or unusual) Revolutionary War sites in America.

Boston, Massachusetts, hometown of Paul Revere, site of the Boston Massacre, the Tea Party, and birthplace of the Revolution. Start at the Visitor Information Booth on Tremont Street, on *Boston Common*, the oldest public park in the East. There you can get free maps, buy public transit tickets, and find out about discount coupons for admission to several historic sites. Walk the *Freedom Trail* through the city, watch videos of Boston's history at the *Old State House*, and stand at the Boston Massacre monument at 30 State Street. Your visit should also include the *Paul Revere House* and *Boston Tea Party Ship and Museum*.

For more suggestions, write to Boston National Historic Park, 15 State Street, Boston, MA 02199, or call free to the Globe Corner Bookstore, built in 1711, at (800) 358-6013. Friendly bookpeople there will suggest guidebooks to consult and offer hints about getting around town.

With Boston, *Philadelphia, Pennsylvania*, shares the birth of the Revolution. You could spend several days here and never run out of historical places to explore. Begin your tour in Old Town, at *Independence National Historical Park*. There are over twenty buildings and sites here, so it is often called "the most historic square mile in America." Because this is a national park, admission to nearly everything is free and open almost every day of the year.

The list that follows describe just a few places you can visit here. But for more information and to make sure you don't miss anything, call or write to Independence National Historical Park, 313 Walnut Street, Philadelphia, PA 19106, (215) 597-8974.

Independence Hall, Chestnut Street between Fifth and and Sixth streets, built as the Pennsylvania State House, became the meeting place for the Second Continental Congress. Most famous as the place where the Declaration of Independence was signed, the rooms are restored right down to quill pens and candles, making them look the way they did when our Founding Fathers spoke here in 1776.

Carpenters' Hall, 320 Chestnut Street, where the First Continental Congress met in 1774, was converted to a hospital for wounded rebel soldiers and later became the first bank building for the United States.

To see military exhibits from the Revolutionary period, visit the *Marine Corps Museum* and the *Army-Navy Museum* near the park visitor's center.

At Market Street between Third and Fourth, don't miss *Franklin Court*. Here an unusual open steel beam model of Franklin's Philadelphia home stands. Below it, underground, is the *Franklin Museum*, with a film and exhibits that show the variety of his genius. If you're curious, pick up a telephone at the video display and call famous historical figures to get their opinions of Franklin.

Graff House, at Seventh and Market streets, has been reconstructed to look as it did when Jefferson rented two rooms there in 1776. You can go upstairs and see them, along with the portable lap desk he invented to use during his "commute" from his home in Virginia to Congress.

Saratoga National Battlefield Park, near Saratoga Springs, New York, in the historic and scenic Hudson River Valley, is where General John Burgoyne surrendered to the Americans in 1777, turning the war in favor of the Americans. The restored battlefield includes a replica of American officers headquarters and a loop road with markers explaining how events turned disastrous for the British.

The visitors' center gives living history demonstrations, displays Revolutionary weapons found there, and shows films dramatizing the battles that signaled the end of British military might in the colonies. Write to Saratoga National Historic Park, Saratoga Springs, NY 12866, (518) 664-9821.

Essex, Connecticut. If they had given a prize for the most amazing military weapon of the war, it surely would have gone to Connecticut's David Bushnell, for designing the *Turtle*. His creation, the world's first submarine, was built in 1775 to attack British ships. It held one man, a bomb, and enough air for a thirty-minute underwater attack. After several failed attempts to destroy British ships, the *Turtle* gave up.

Start your tour in Essex, at the Connecticut River Museum on Steamboat Dock, (213) 767-8289. See the working model of the *Turtle* and other maritime history displays. At Railroad Avenue, during good weather months, you can hop aboard a steam locomotive for a nine-mile train ride into the nearby countryside. When you detrain at Deep River, your tour takes you next onto a riverboat that runs up and down the Connecticut River, while you hear stories of nearby history. Your three-hour trip ends with a train-ride back to Essex.

Across the street from the maritime museum, at 48 Main, visit the Griswold Inn, built in 1776 and still an inn and tavern today. Write for more information from the Connecticut Valley Tourism Commission, 393 Main Street, Middletown, CT 06457.

As you think about these historic places and the events that led to the American Revolution, remember that your freedom is a gift from the hundreds of men and women, both ordinary and famous, who courageously fought for the right to rule themselves in 1776.

Index

Adams, John, 63, 65–66
Adams, Samuel, 26, 27, 31, 34–35, 42
Arnold, Commander Benedict, 74
Attucks, Crispus, 28–31

Boone, Daniel, 50–51, 53
Boston Massacre: A Play, 28–31
Boston Tea Party, 31–34
Breed's Hill, Battle of, 48–49
Bunker Hill, Battle of, 49
Burgoyne, General John, 76, 78, 83

Clinton, General Henry, 49, 81
Colonies, Map of the Thirteen, 14
Committees of Correspondence, 31, 46
Common Sense, 58, 59
Concord, 38–47
Congress: First Continental, 34–35; Second Continental, 61, 63; Stamp Act, 27, 34–35
Cornwallis, General, 89–91, 93–94

Dawes, William, 39, 42
Declaration of Independence, 61–63, 65–66, 67
Dunlap, John, 63

Flags, 82–83
Fourth of July, 63–65
France, 79, 81, 91
Franklin, Benjamin, 54–56, 63, 66, 79

Gage, General Thomas, 37–38, 48
George (King of England), 7, 37, 54, 58, 66
Goddard, Mary Katharine, 66

Hancock, John, 42, 63
Howe, Admiral Richard, 66
Howe, General William, 48–49, 66, 69, 77, 81
Howe, John, 37–38

Indentured servants, 58

Jefferson, Thomas, 61–63

Lafayette, General, 90–91
Lafayette, James Armistead, 91
Lee, Richard Henry, 62–63
Lexington, 38–39, 43, 46–47
Lincoln, General Benjamin, 89, 94
Lovell, General Solomon, 85–86

Malcolm, Captain John, 23
Martin, Joseph Plumb, 72–74, 78
Mechanics, 36–39
Militia, 11, 43, 46–49, 69–71, 73
Monmouth, Battle of, 81

O'Hara, Brigadier General Charles, 94

Paine, Thomas, 59
Palmer, Joseph, 46–47
Penobscot Bay, Battle of, 85–87
Pirates, 81, 84–88
Pitcairn, Major, 43, 48–49
Prescott, Colonel, 48–49

Quakers, 68–71

Revere, Paul, 28, 35–37, 39, 42, 85
Robinson, John, 21
Ross, Betsy, 82

Saltonstall, Captain Dudley, 85–87
Slaves, 28–31, 51, 57–58, 91
Sons of Liberty, 24, 26–27, 35–36
Spain, 82, 89
Spies, 36–39, 91
Stamp Act, 22, 24–25, 27
Suffolk Resolve, 34–35

Trask, Israel, 84–87
Turtle, 88

Valley Forge, 77–79, 81, 89

Warren, 85–86
Washington, General George, 47, 55, 58, 66, 69, 70, 74–75, 77–79, 81, 93–94
Wheatley, Phillis, 57–58
Wister, Sarah, 68–71
Women in Battle, 89

Yankee Doodle, 10
Yorktown, Battle of, 90–91